E-Z PLAY TODAY 5 — ALL-TIME STANDARDS

ISBN 0-7935-3682-0

HAL•LEONARD CORPORATION

7777 W. BLUEMOUND RD. P.O. BOX 13819 MILWAUKEE, WI 53213

Anniversary Song

Registration 6
Rhythm: Waltz

By Al Jolson
and Saul Chaplin

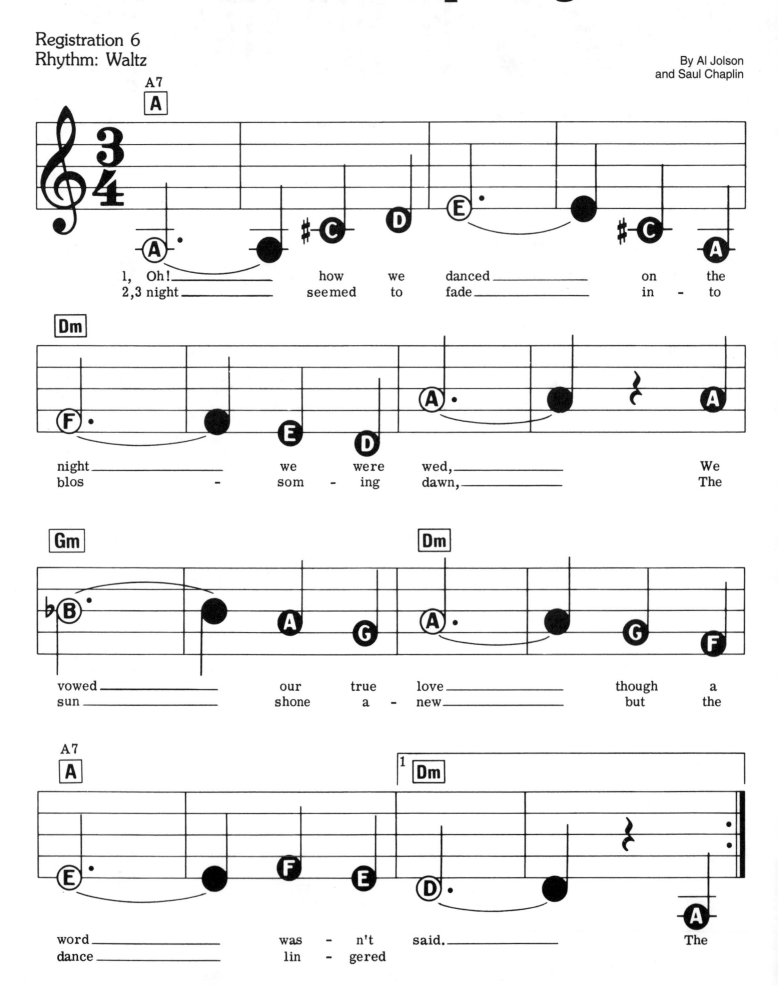

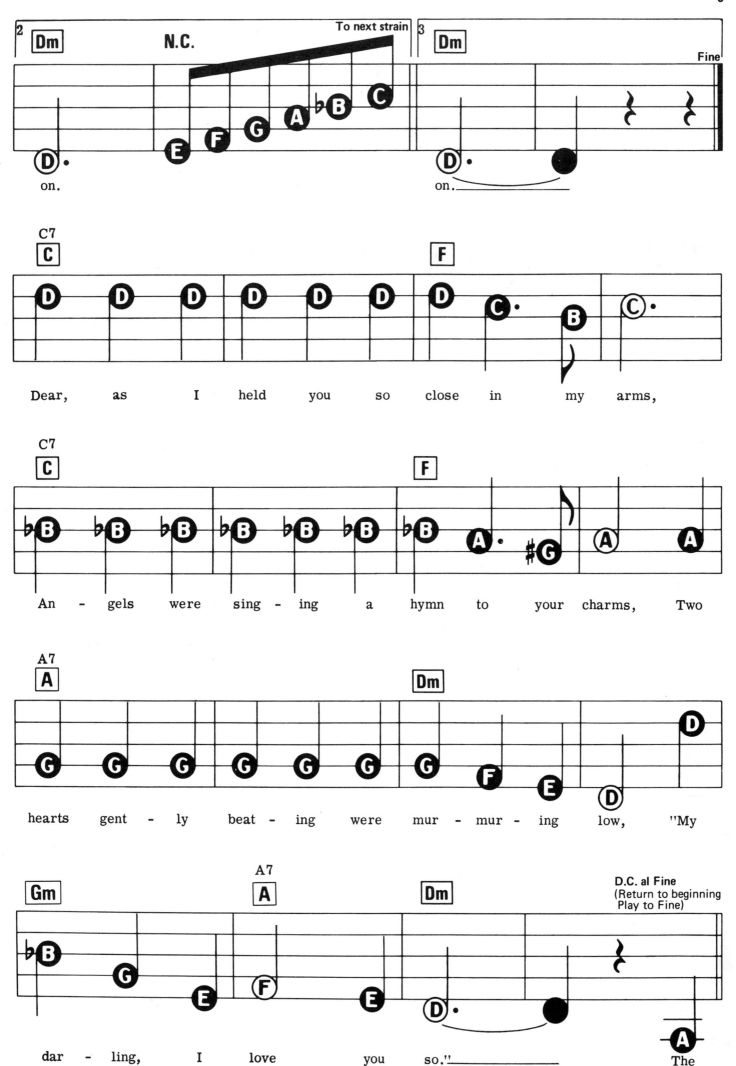

Dear, as I held you so close in my arms,

An - gels were sing - ing a hymn to your charms, Two

hearts gent - ly beat - ing were mur - mur - ing low, "My

dar - ling, I love you so." The

Baby, Won't You Please Come Home

Words and Music by Charles Warfield
and Clarence Williams

Registration 7
Rhythm: Fox Trot or Swing

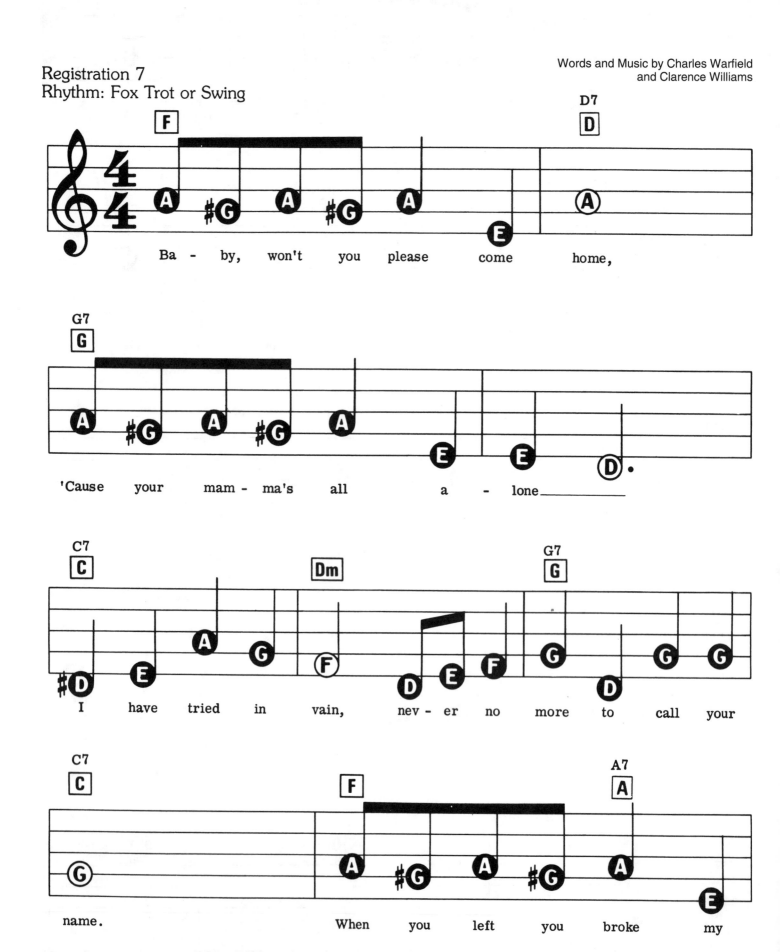

Beyond The Blue Horizon

Registration 3
Rhythm: Fox-Trot or Rock

Words by Leo Robin
Music by Richard A. Whiting and W. Franke Harling

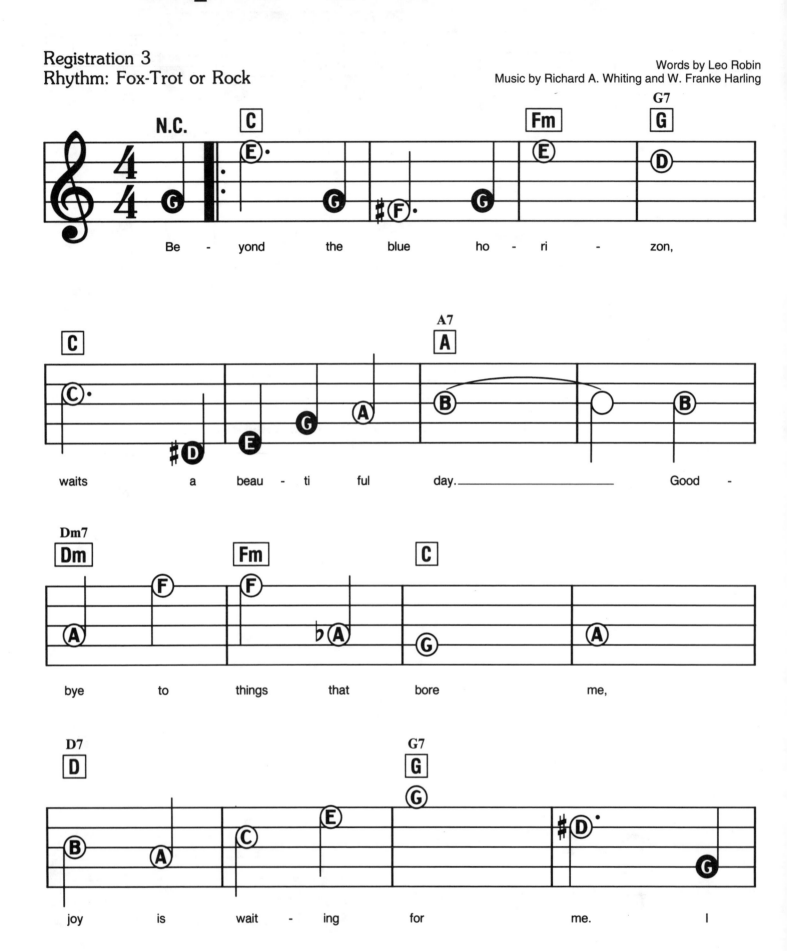

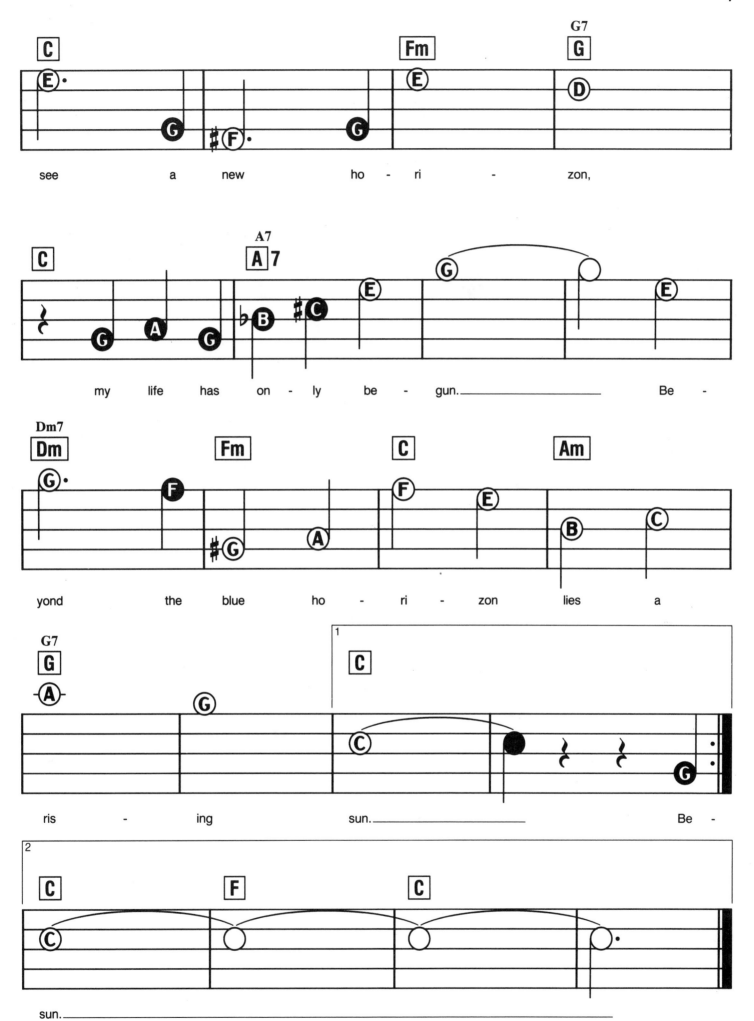

Everybody Loves My Baby
(But My Baby Don't Love Nobody But Me)

Registration 5
Rhythm: Swing or Fox Trot

Words and Music by Jack Palmer
and Spencer Williams

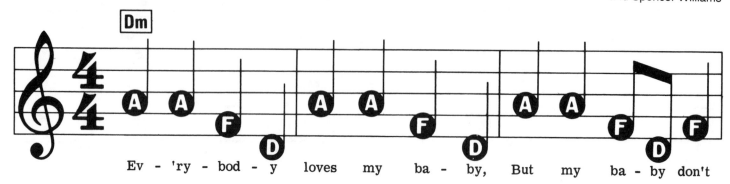

Ev - 'ry - bod - y loves my ba - by, But my ba - by don't

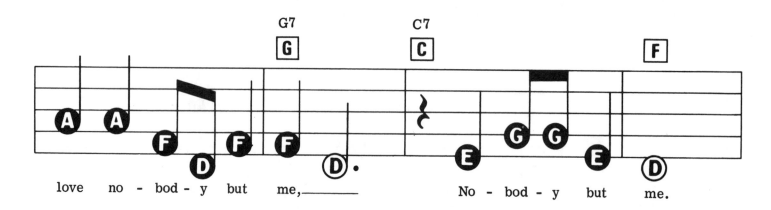

love no - bod - y but me,_____ No - bod - y but me.

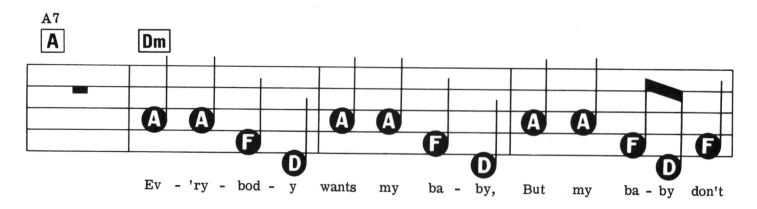

Ev - 'ry - bod - y wants my ba - by, But my ba - by don't

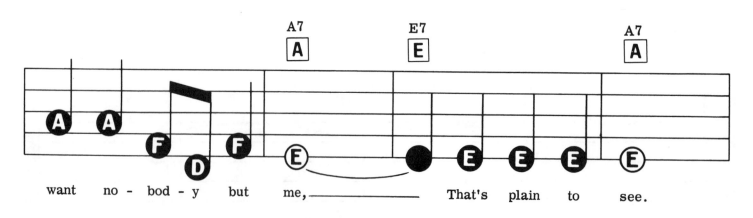

want no - bod - y but me,_____ That's plain to see.

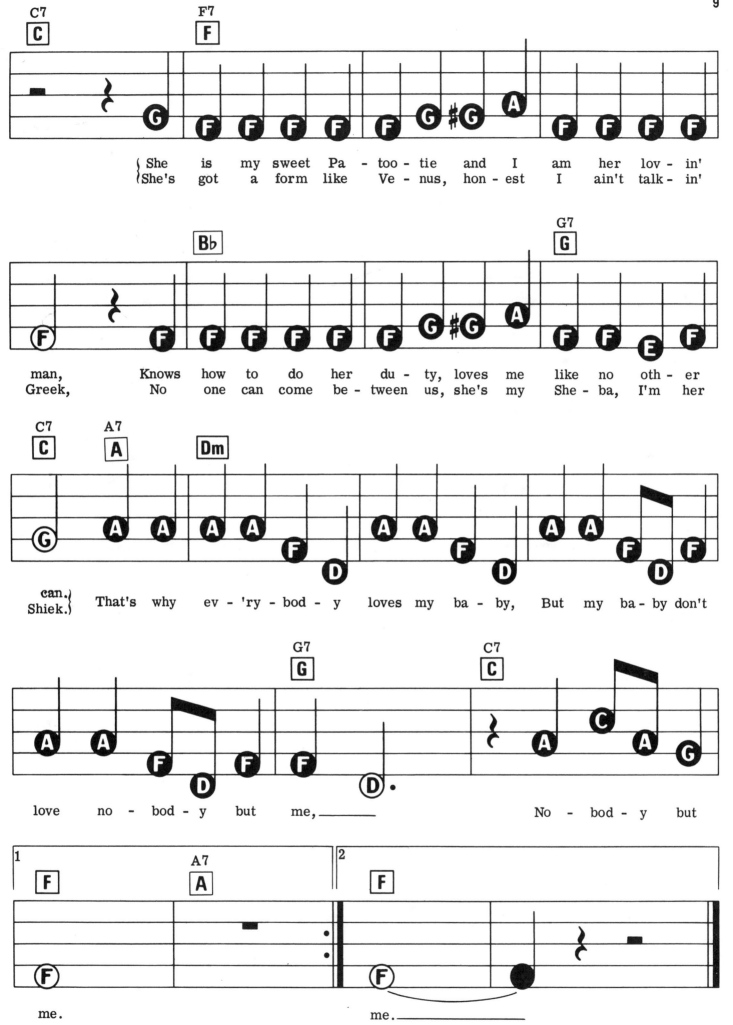

(I Love You)
For Sentimental Reasons

Registration 1
Rhythm: Fox Trot or Swing

Words by Deek Watson
Music by William Best

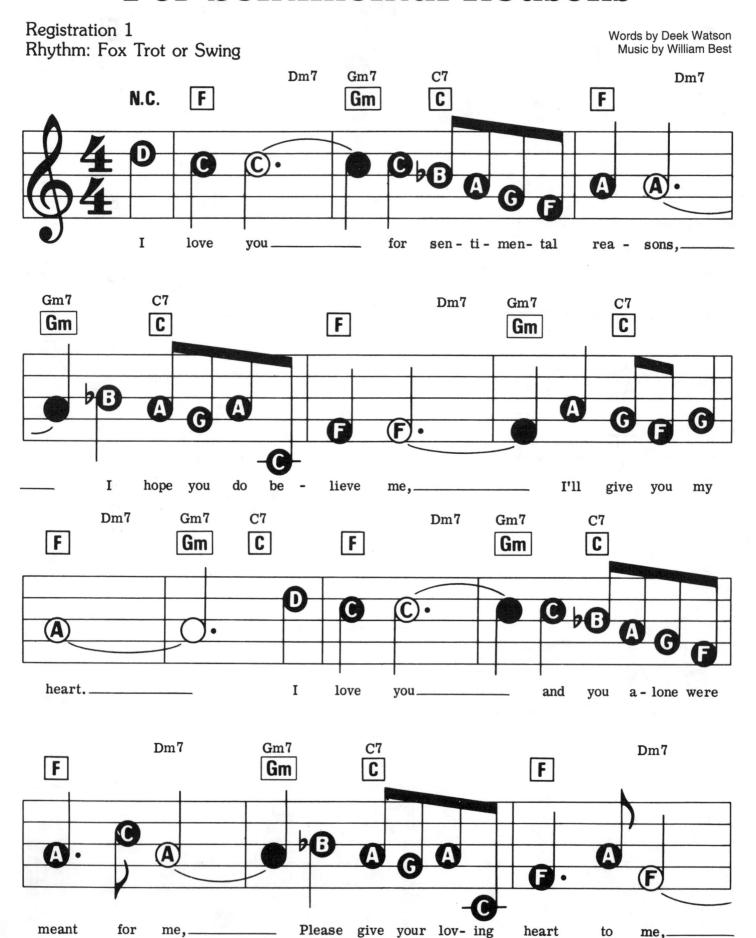

MCA music publishing

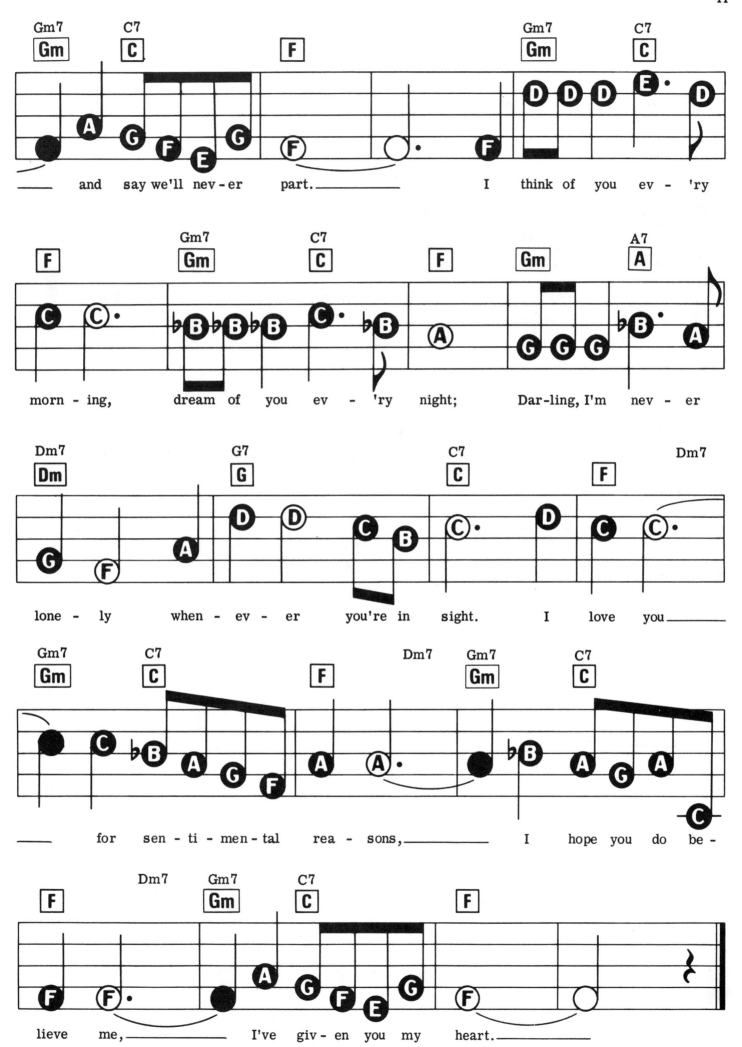

Harlem Nocturne

Registration 2
Rhythm: Swing or Jazz

Words by Dick Rogers
Music by Earle Hagen

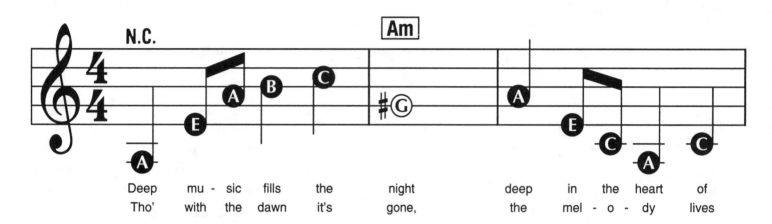

Deep mu - sic fills the night, deep in the heart of
Tho' with the dawn it's gone, the mel - o - dy lives

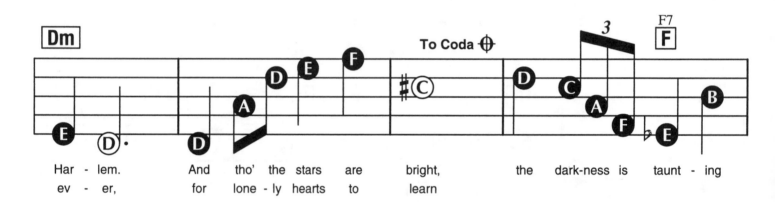

Har - lem. And tho' the stars are bright, the dark-ness is taunt - ing
ev - er, for lone - ly hearts to learn

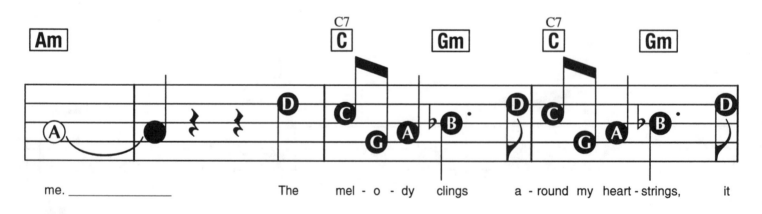

me. _____ The mel - o - dy clings a - round my heart - strings, it

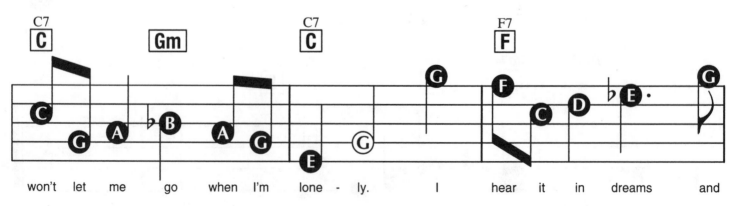

won't let me go when I'm lone - ly. I hear it in dreams and

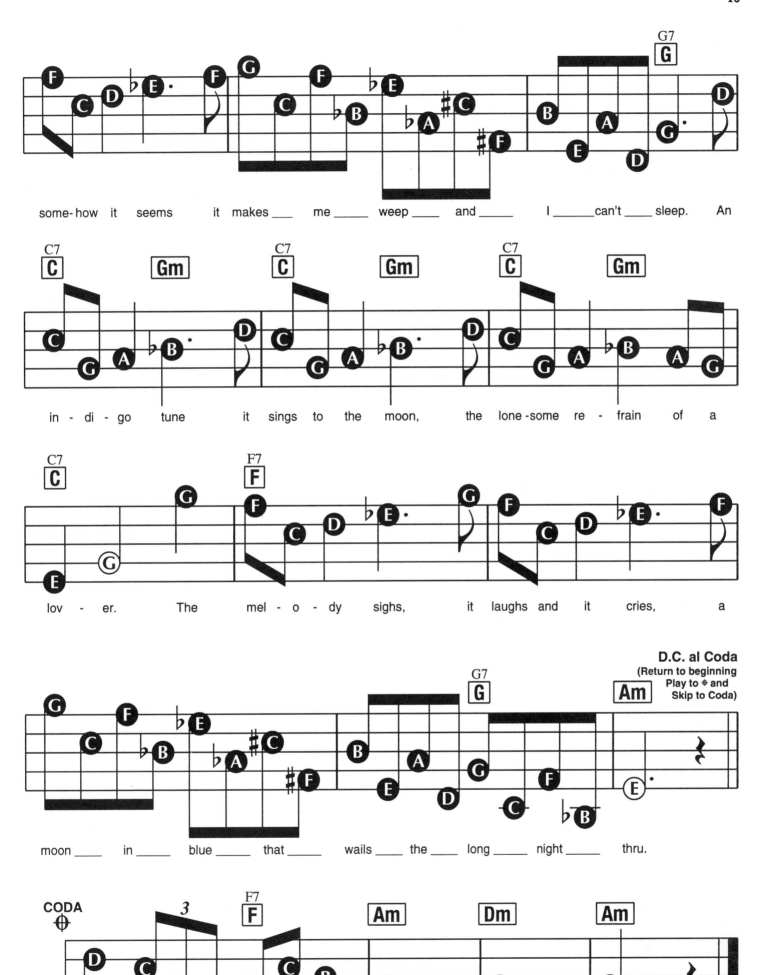

some-how it seems it makes ___ me ___ weep ___ and ___ I ___ can't ___ sleep. An

in - di - go tune it sings to the moon, the lone -some re - frain of a

lov - er. The mel - o - dy sighs, it laughs and it cries, a

D.C. al Coda
(Return to beginning
Play to ⊕ and
Skip to Coda)

moon ___ in ___ blue ___ that ___ wails ___ the ___ long ___ night ___ thru.

CODA

of love in a Har - lem noc - turne. _____

The Hawaiian Wedding Song
(Ke Kali Nei Au)

Registration 10
Rhythm: Ballad or Slow Rock

English Lyrics by Al Hoffman and Dick Manning
Hawaiian Lyrics and Music by Charles E. King

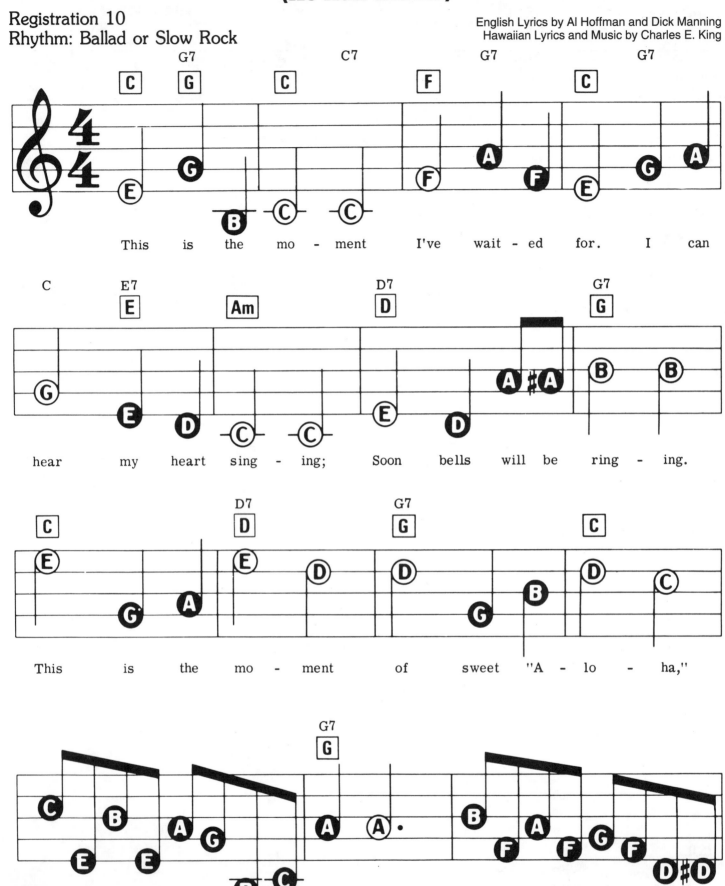

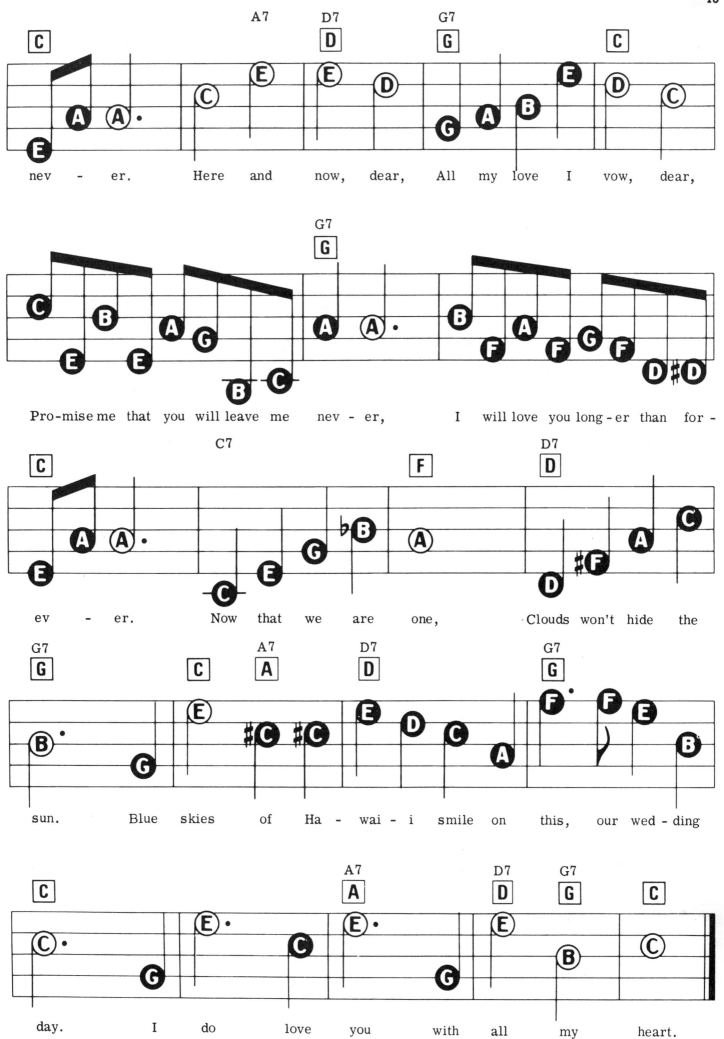

Heart And Soul

Registration 8
Rhythm: Swing

Words by Frank Loesser
Music by Hoagy Carmichael

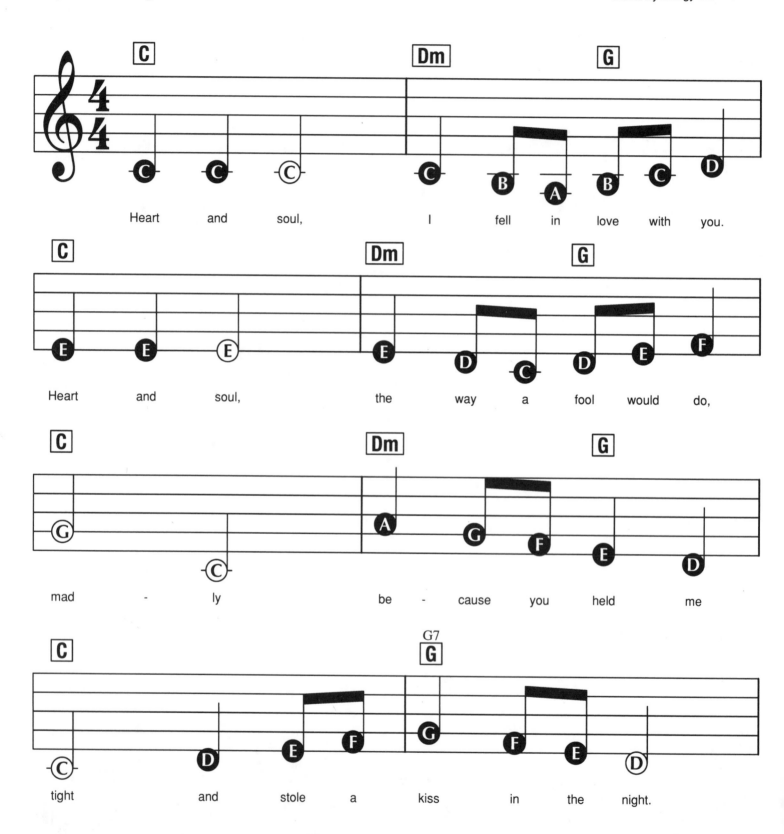

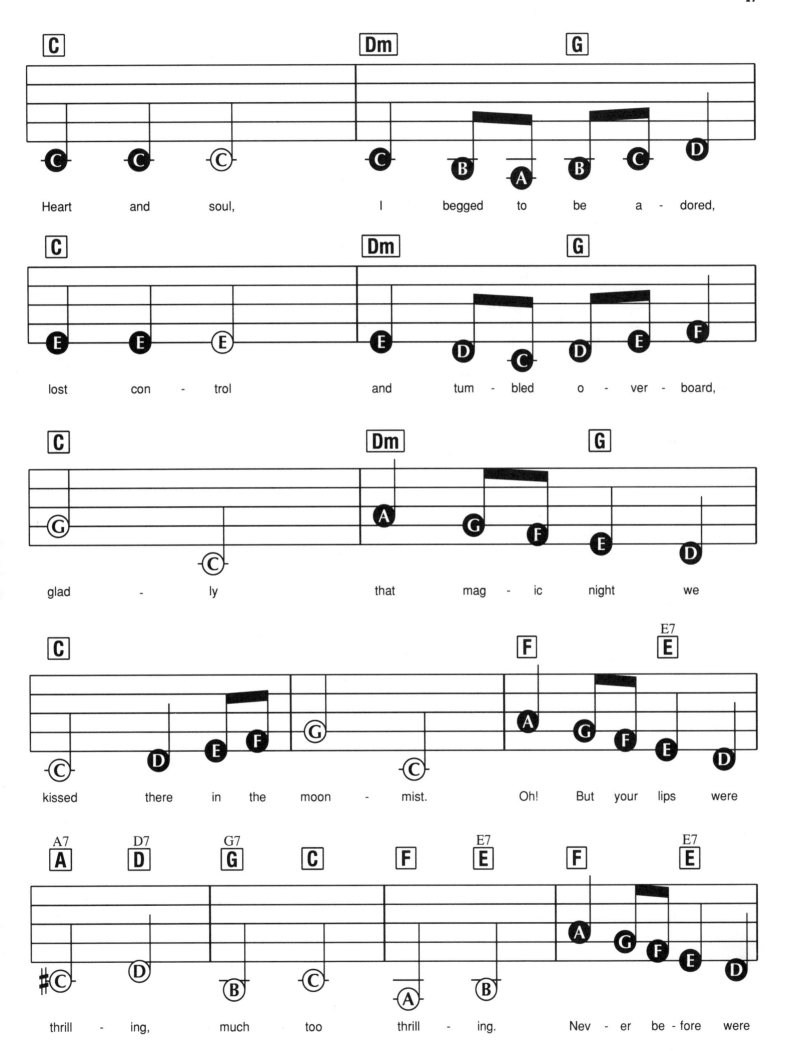

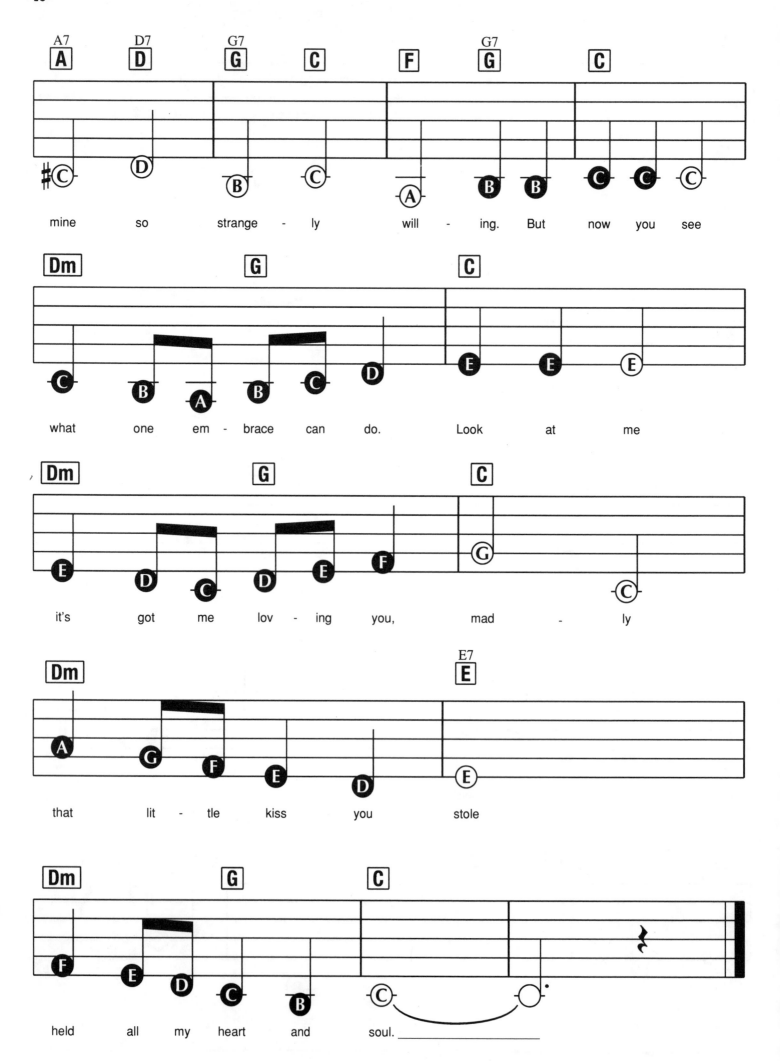

More Than You Know

Registration 8
Rhythm: Fox Trot

Words by William Rose and Edward Eliscu
Music by Vincent Youmans

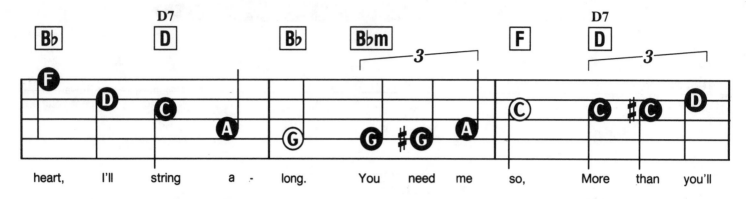

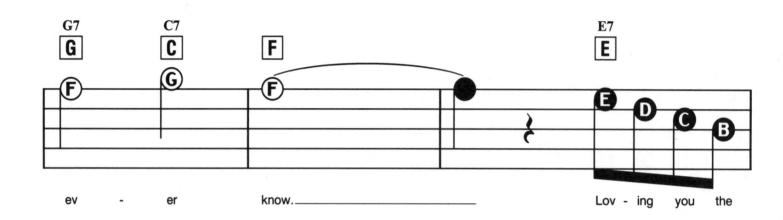

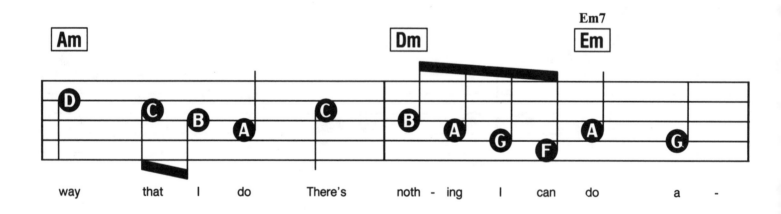

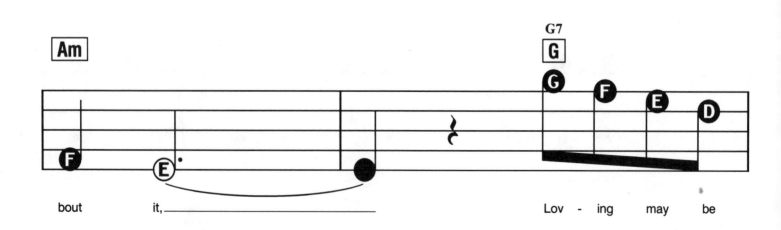

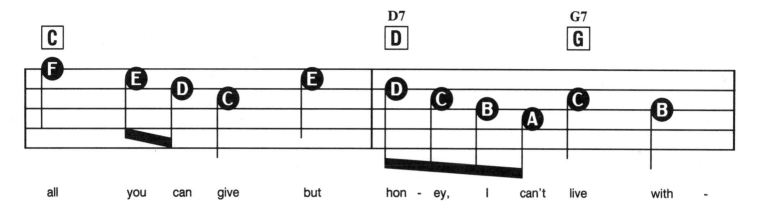

all you can give but hon - ey, I can't live with -

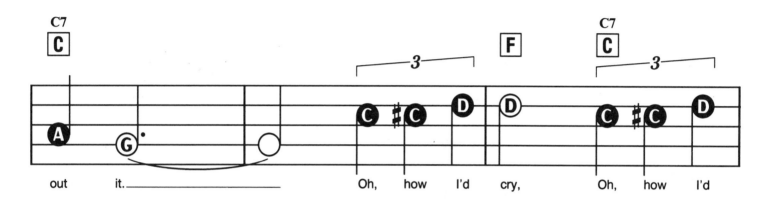

out it. Oh, how I'd cry, Oh, how I'd

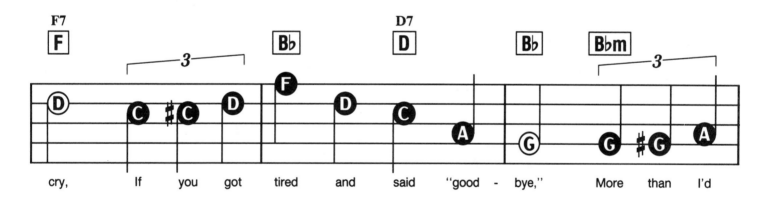

cry, If you got tired and said "good - bye," More than I'd

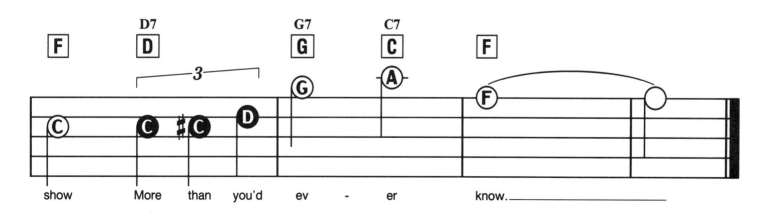

show More than you'd ev - er know.

I Don't Want To Walk Without You

Registration 1
Rhythm: Swing

Words by Frank Loesser
Music by Jule Styne

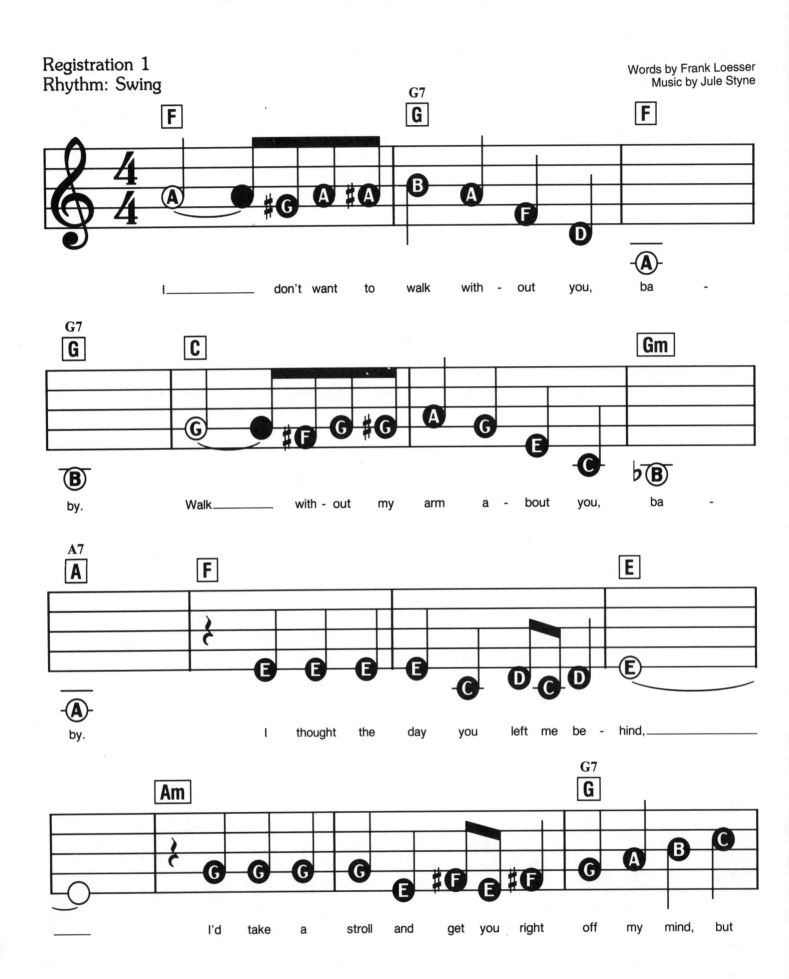

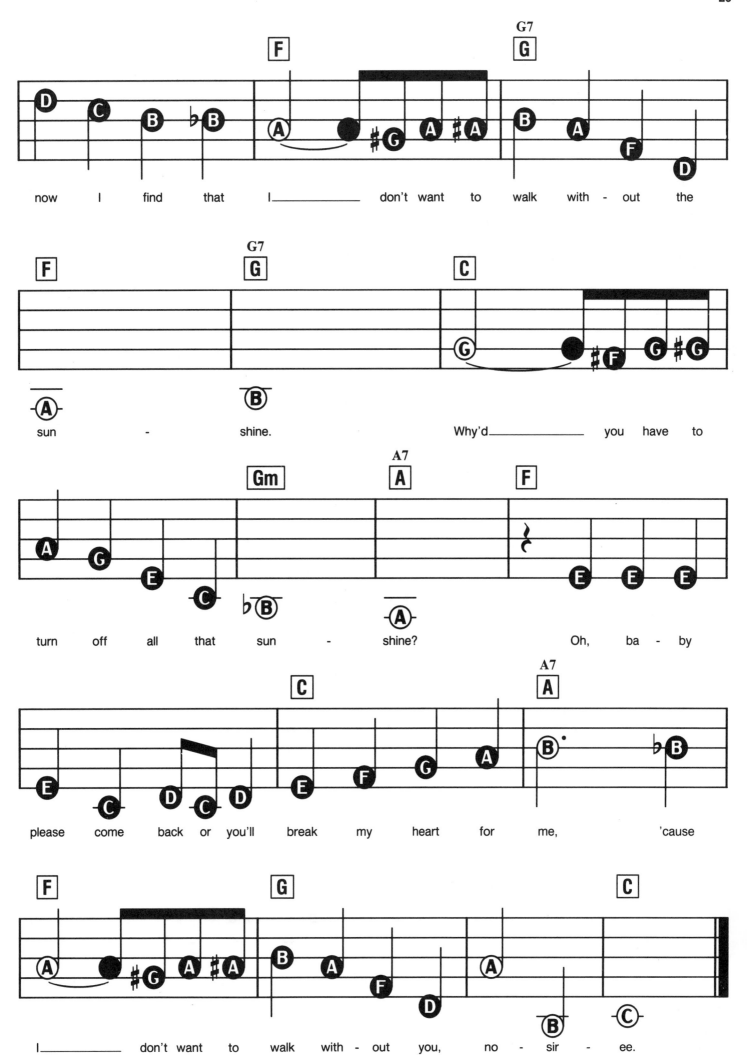

Just Because

Registration 5
Rhythm: Polka or March

Words and Music by Bob and Joe Shelton
and Sid Robin

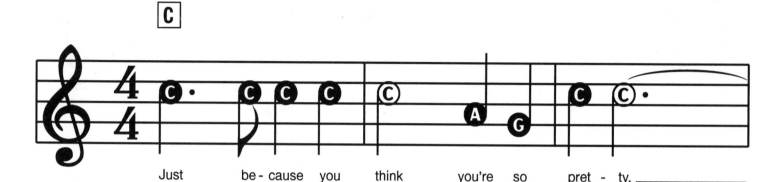

Just be - cause you think you're so pret - ty, _____

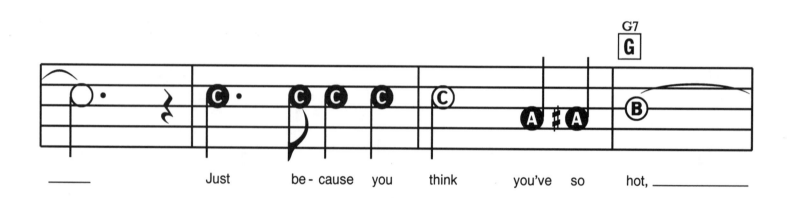

_____ Just be - cause you think you've so hot, _____

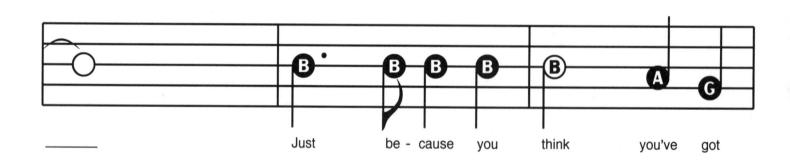

_____ Just be - cause you think you've got

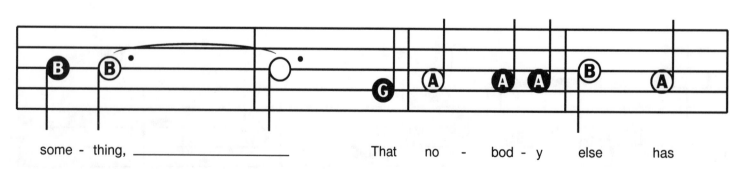

some - thing, _____ That no - bod - y else has

MCA music publishing

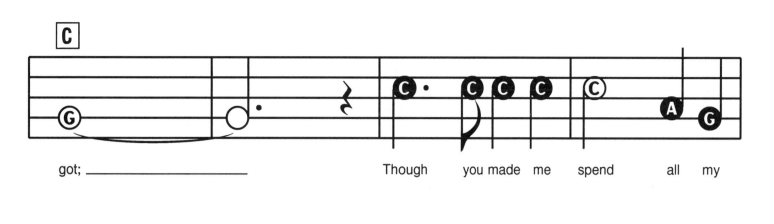

got; _____ Though you made me spend all my

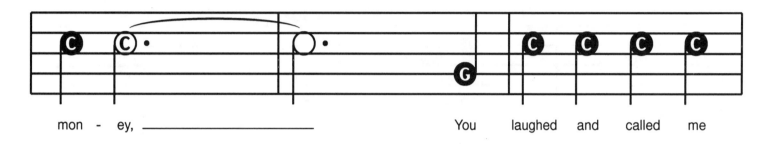

mon - ey, _____ You laughed and called me

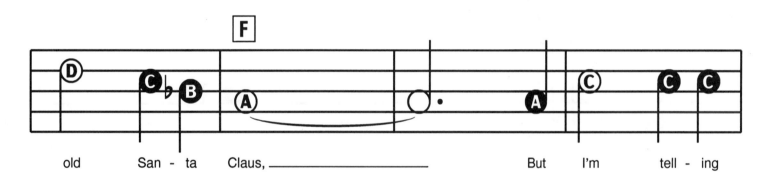

old San - ta Claus, _____ But I'm tell - ing

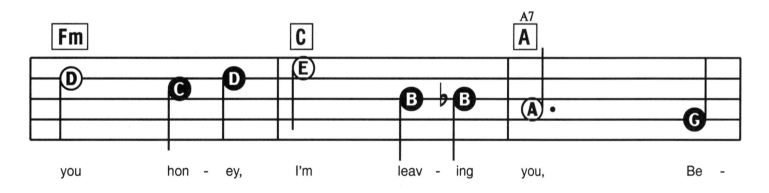

you hon - ey, I'm leav - ing you, Be -

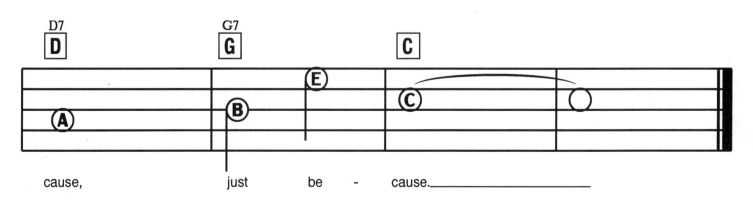

cause, just be - cause._____

Just One More Chance

Registration 4
Rhythm: Swing

Words by Sam Coslow
Music by Arthur Johnston

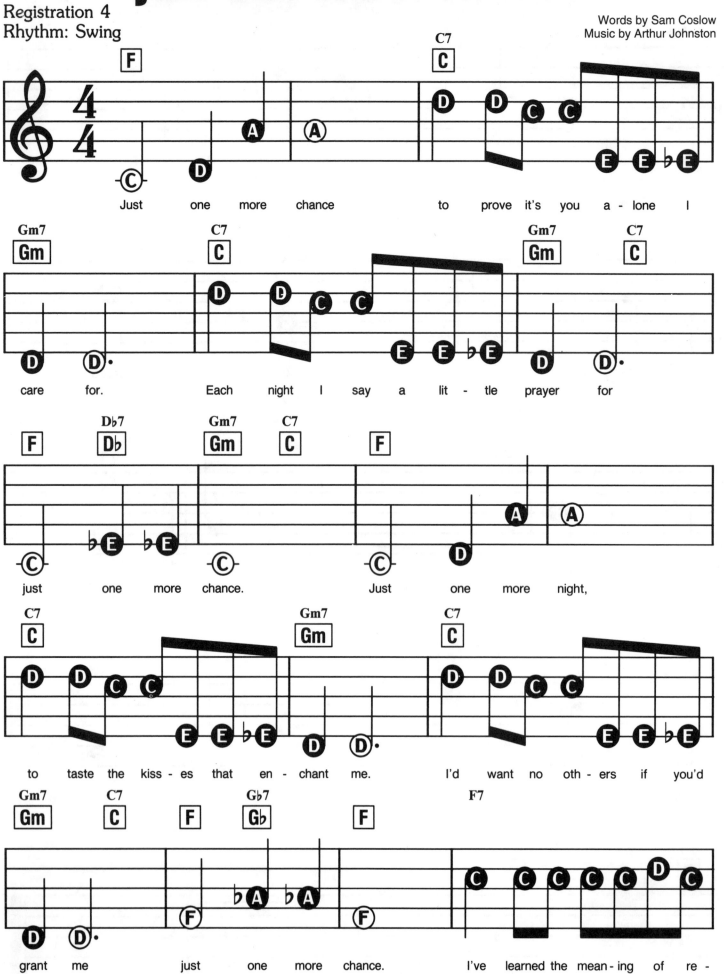

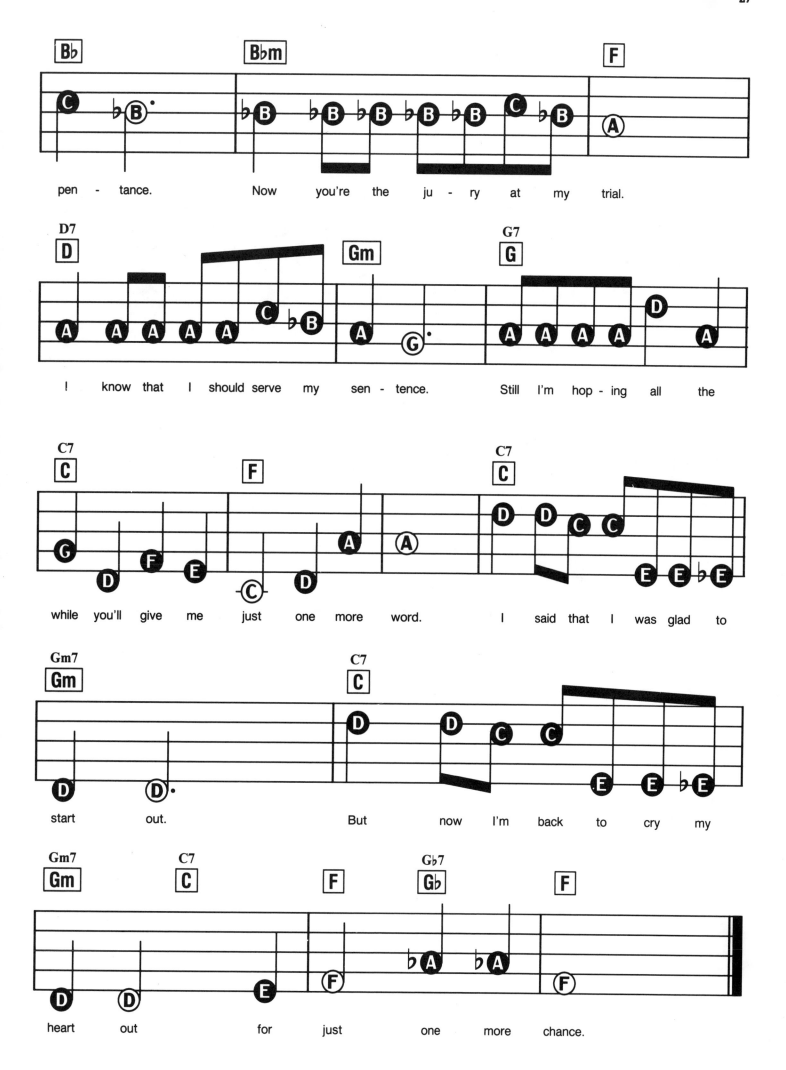

Louise

Registration 7
Rhythm: Swing or Shuffle

Words by Leo Robin
Music by Richard A. Whiting

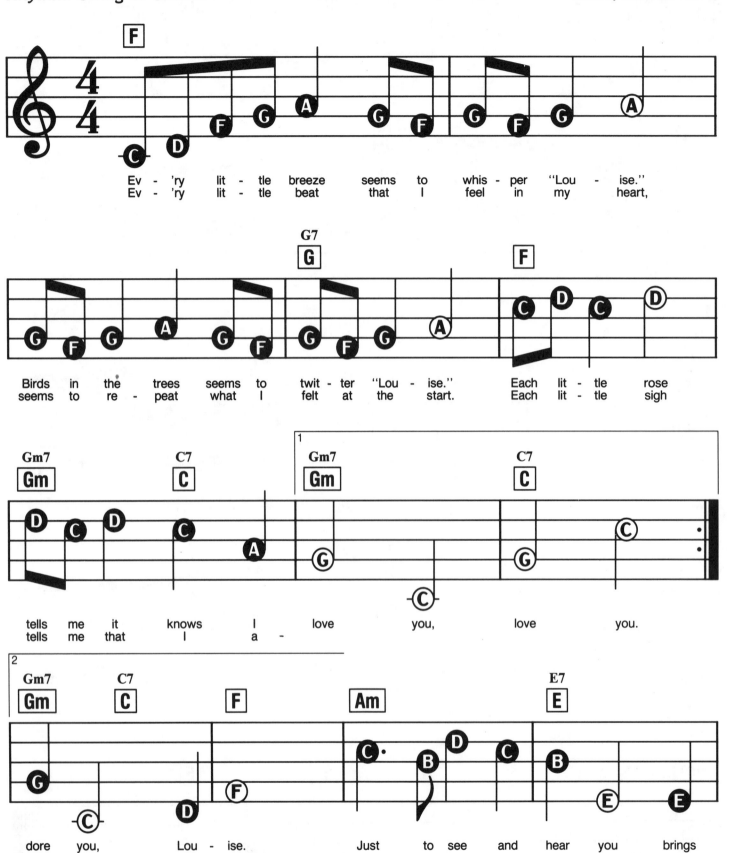

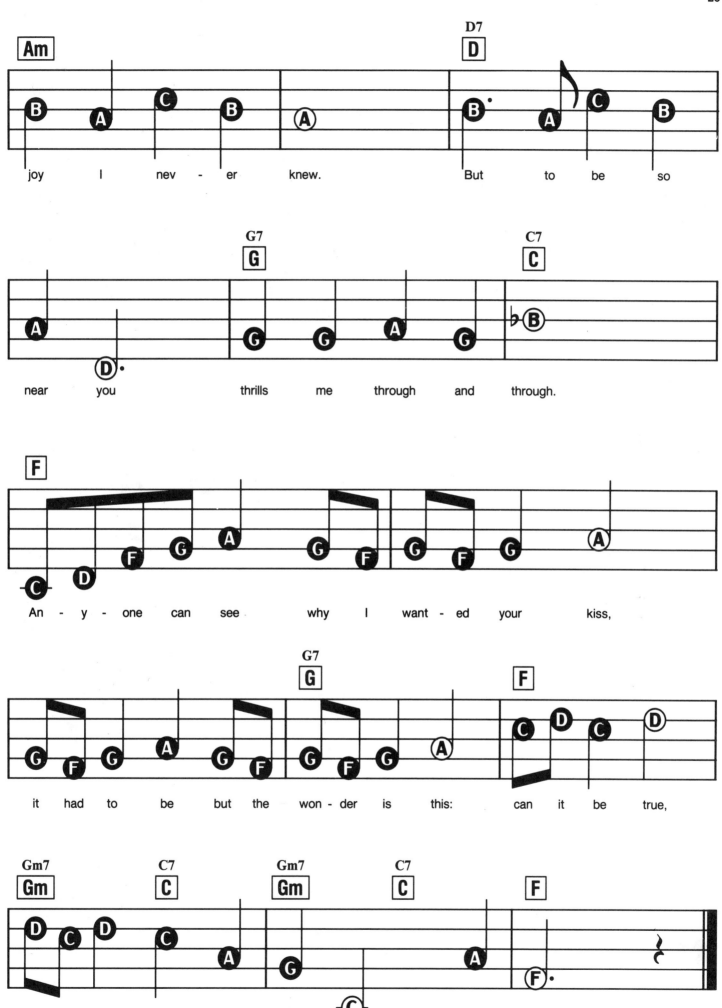

L-O-V-E

Registration 8
Rhythm: Fox Trot or Swing

Words and Music by Bert Kaempfert
and Milt Gabler

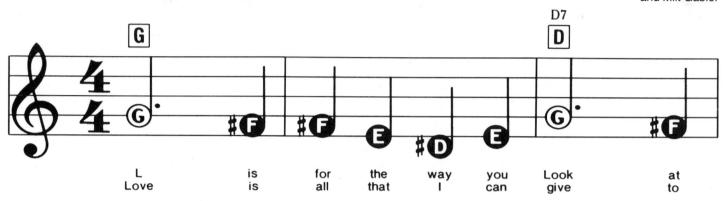

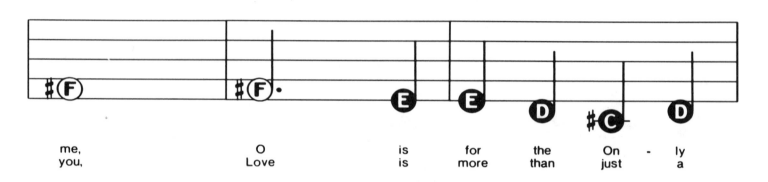

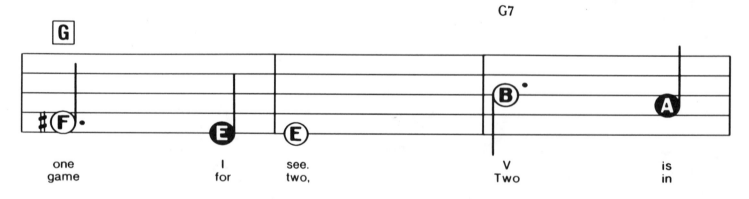

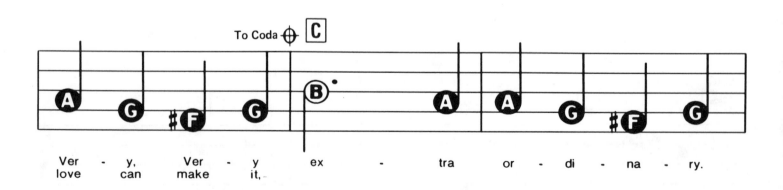

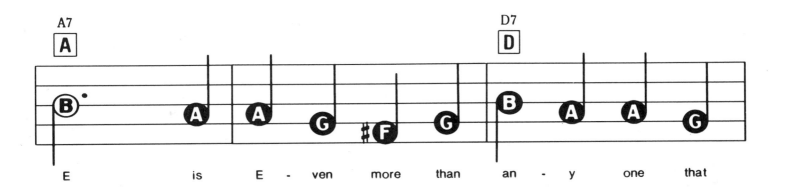

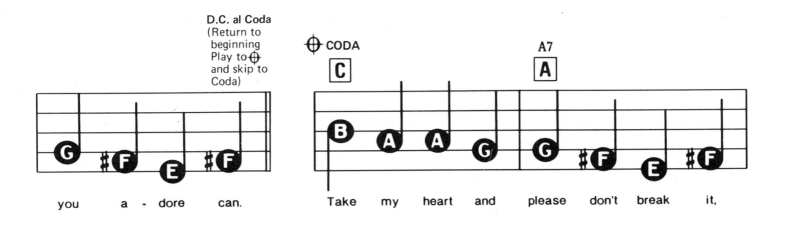

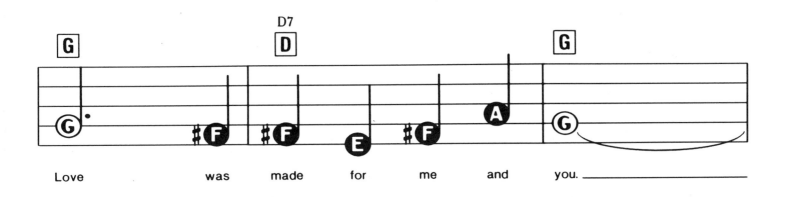

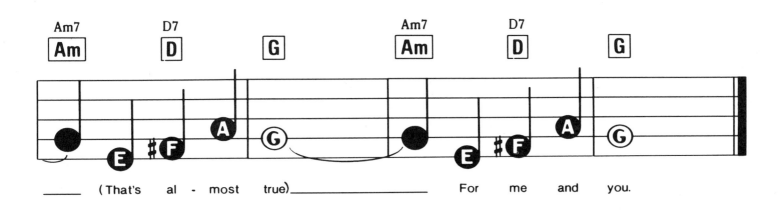

A Man Without Love
(Quando M'Innamoro)

Registration 8
Rhythm: Fox Trot or Swing

English Words by Barry Mason
Original Words and Music by D. Pace, M. Panzeri and R. Livraghi

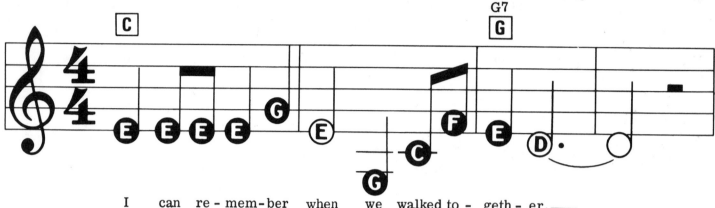

I can re-mem-ber when we walked to-geth-er,_____

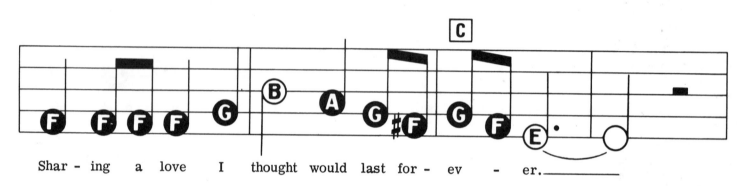

Shar-ing a love I thought would last for-ev-er._____

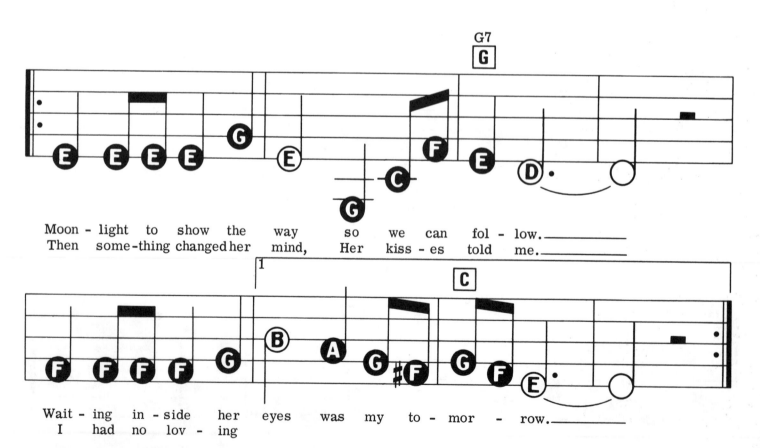

Moon-light to show the way so we can fol-low._____
Then some-thing changed her mind, Her kiss-es told me._____

Wait-ing in-side her eyes was my to-mor-row._____
I had no lov-ing

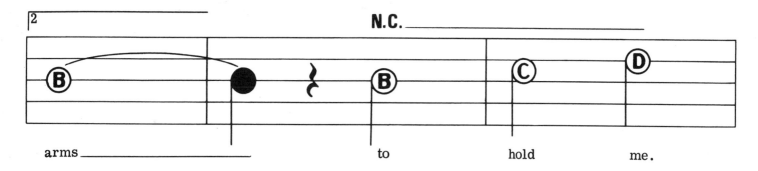

arms_____ to hold me.

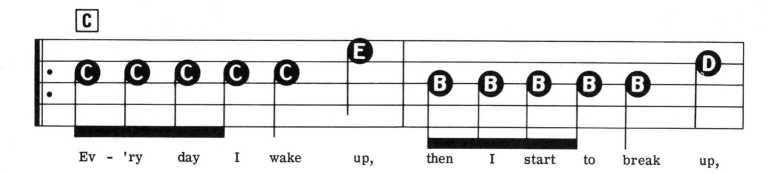

Ev - 'ry day I wake up, then I start to break up,

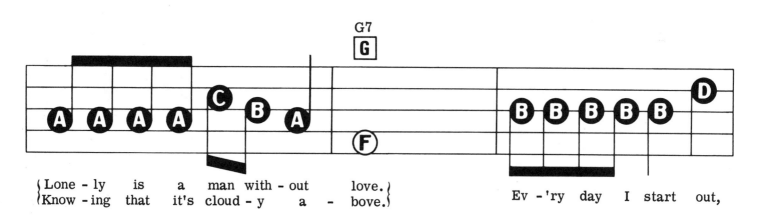

{Lone - ly is a man with - out love.}
{Know - ing that it's cloud - y a - bove.} Ev -'ry day I start out,

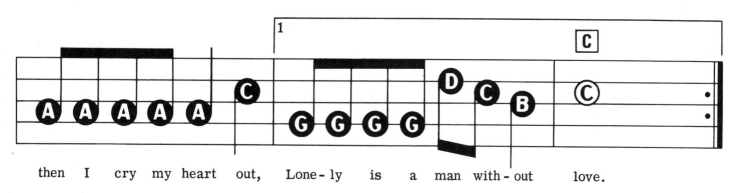

then I cry my heart out, Lone - ly is a man with - out love.

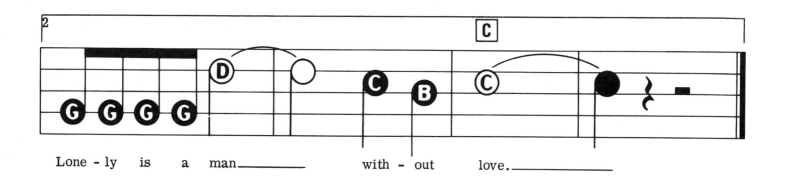

Lone - ly is a man_____ with - out love._____

Memories Of You

Registration 9
Rhythm: Fox Trot or Swing

Lyrics by Andy Razaf
Music by Eubie Blake

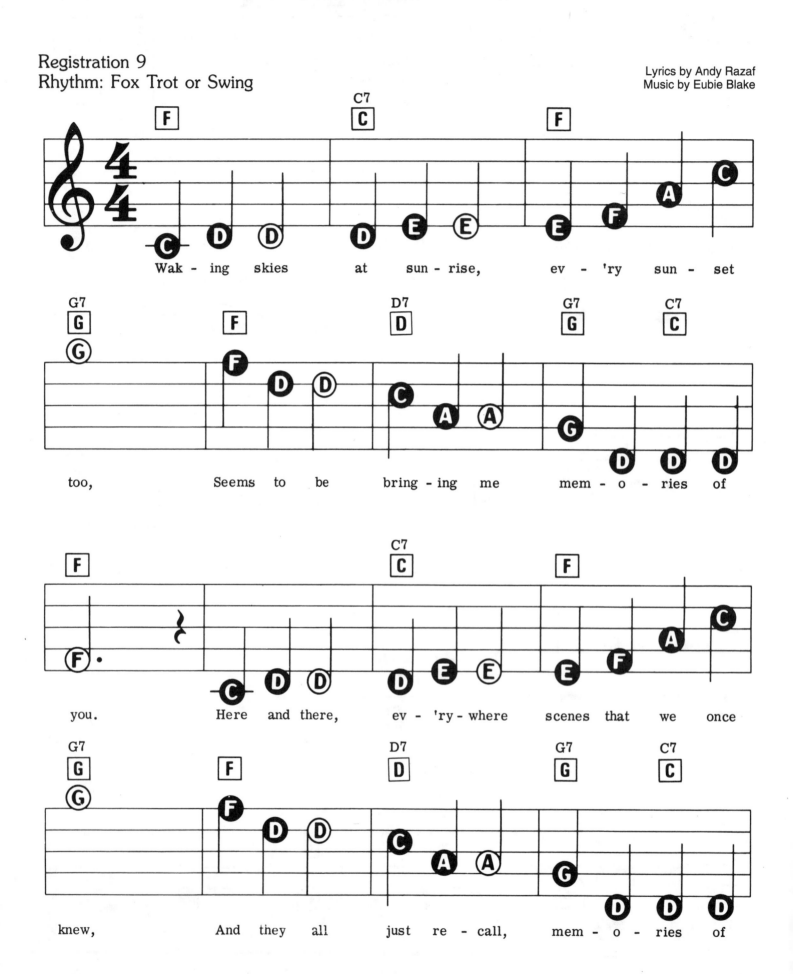

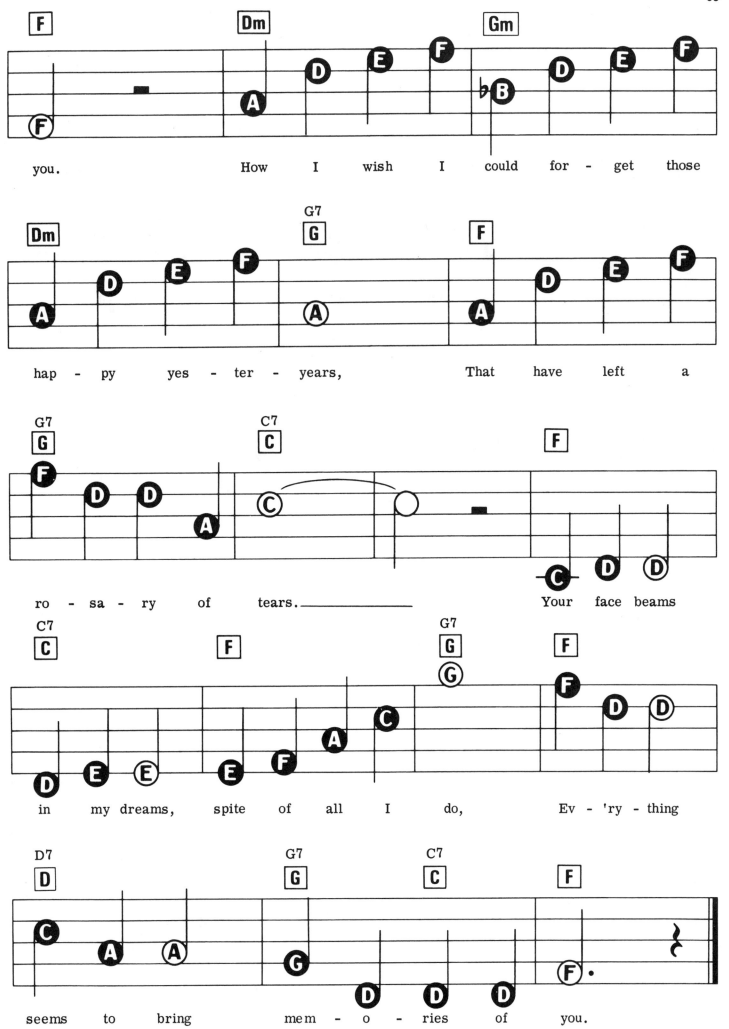

Que Sera, Sera
(Whatever Will Be, Will Be)

Registration 10
Rhythm: Waltz

Words and Music by Jay Livingston
and Ray Evans

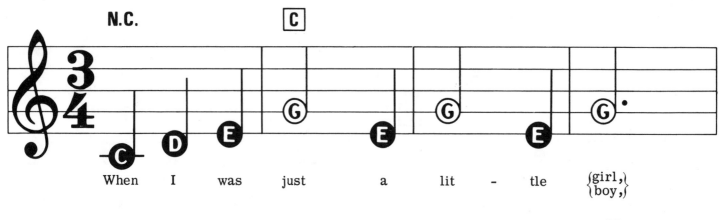

When I was just a lit - tle {girl,} {boy,}

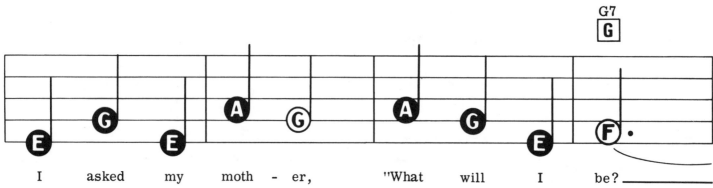

I asked my moth - er, "What will I be? _____

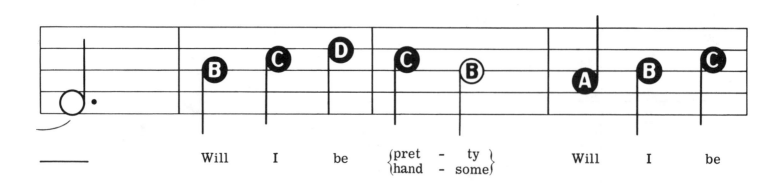

_____ Will I be {pret - ty } {hand - some} Will I be

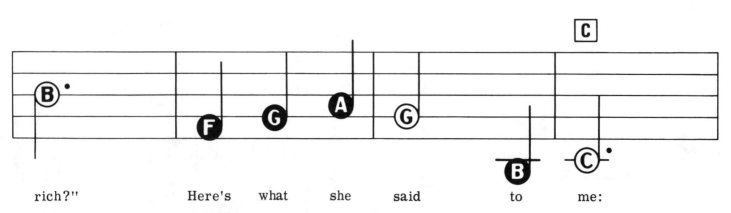

rich?" Here's what she said to me:

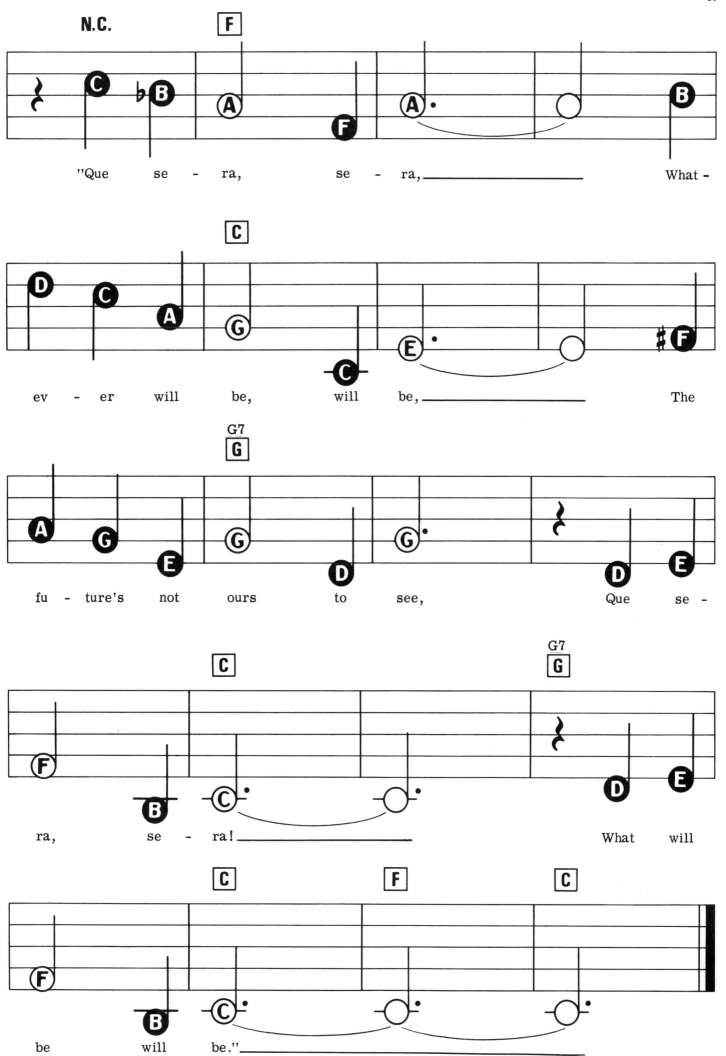

Song Of The Islands

Registration 3
Rhythm: Fox Trot or Swing

Words and Music by
Charles E. King

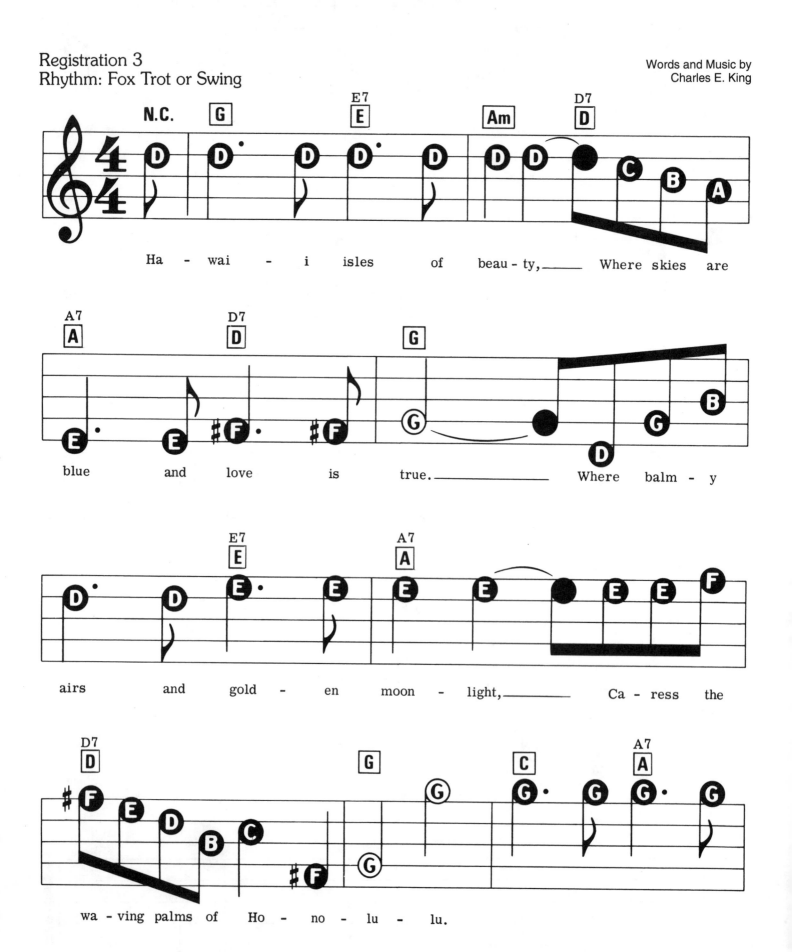

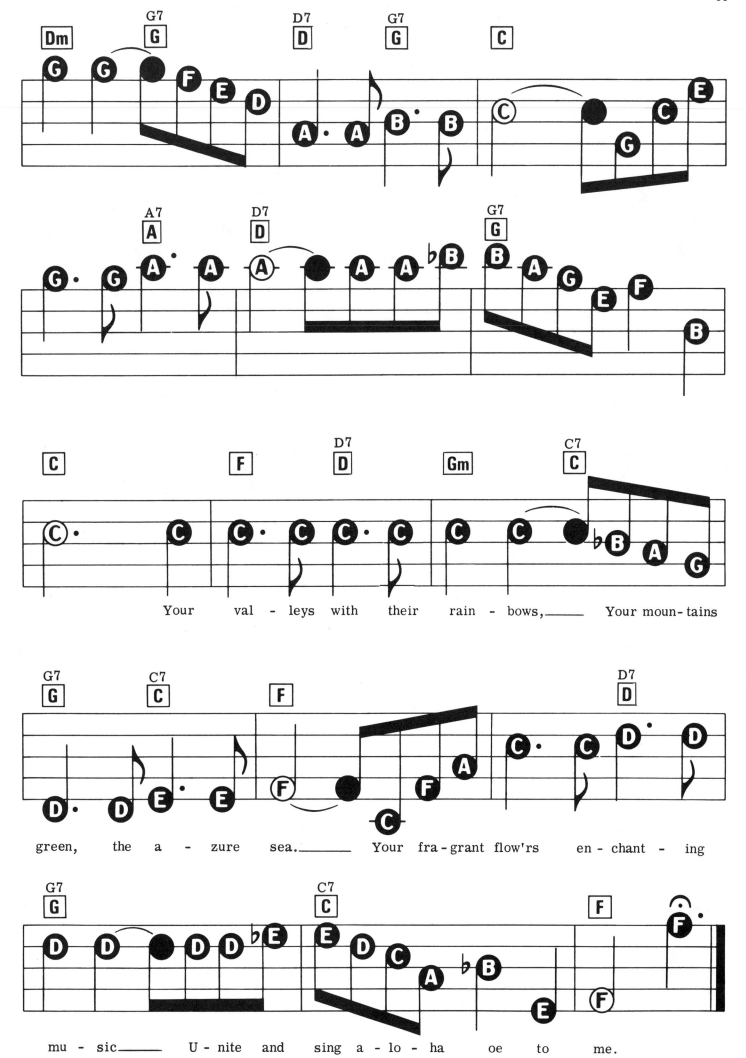

Your val - leys with their rain - bows,_____ Your moun - tains

green, the a - zure sea._____ Your fra - grant flow'rs en - chant - ing

mu - sic_____ U - nite and sing a - lo - ha oe to me.

Tangerine

Registration 9
Rhythm: Pops or Latin

Words by Johnny Mercer
Music by Victor Schertzinger

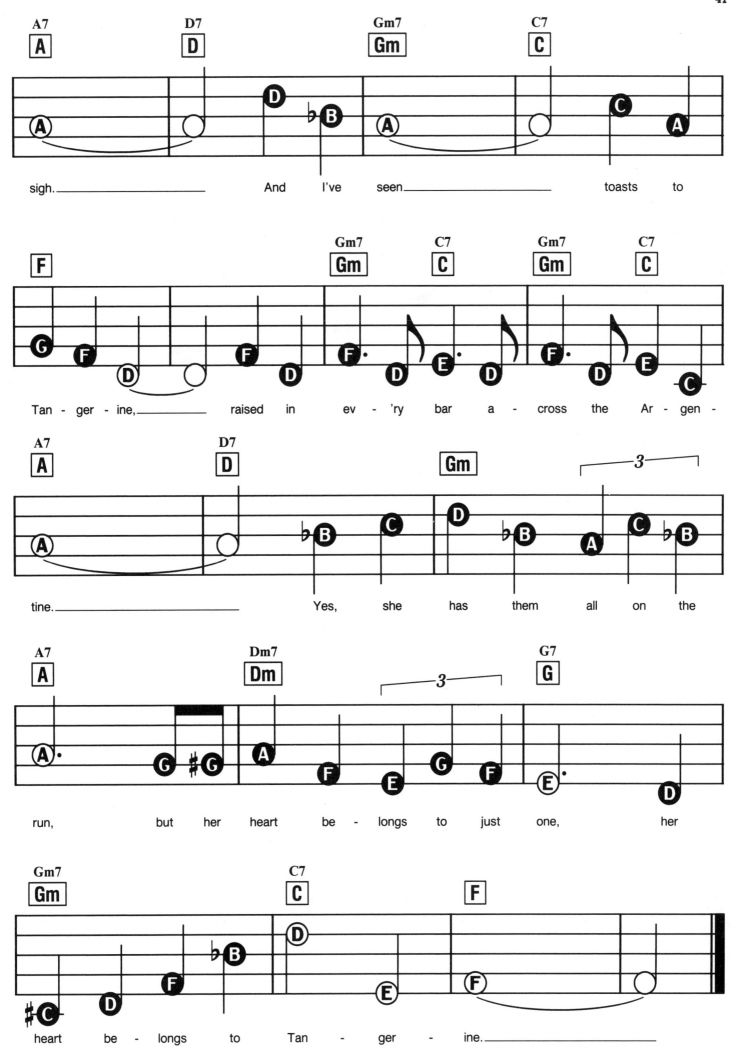

Thanks For The Memory

Registration 3
Rhythm: Swing

Words and Music by Leo Robin
and Ralph Rainger

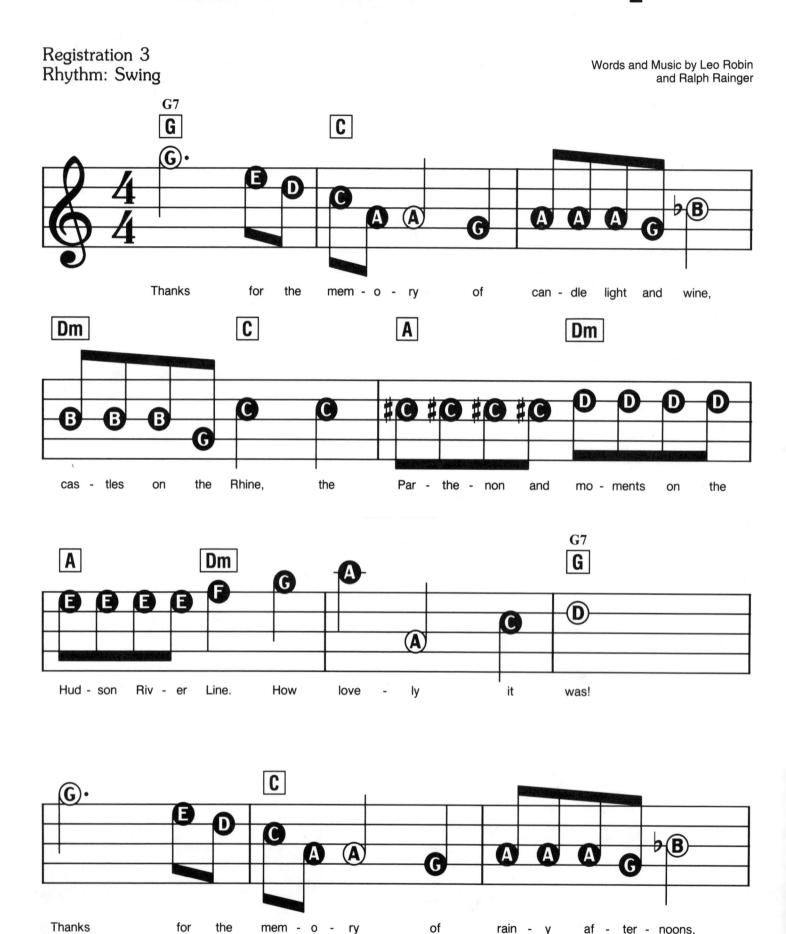

43

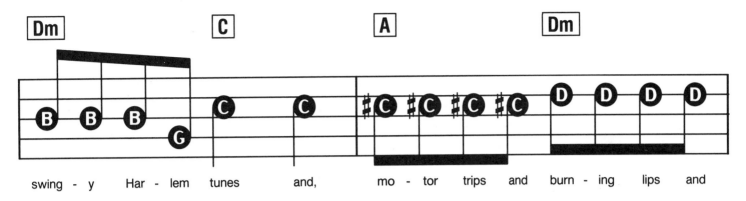

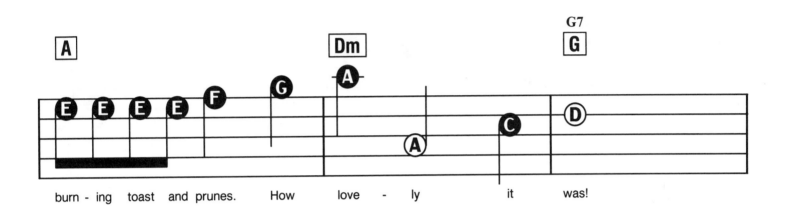

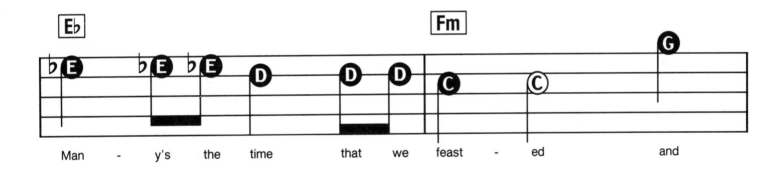

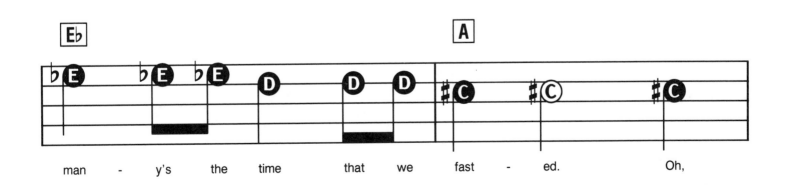

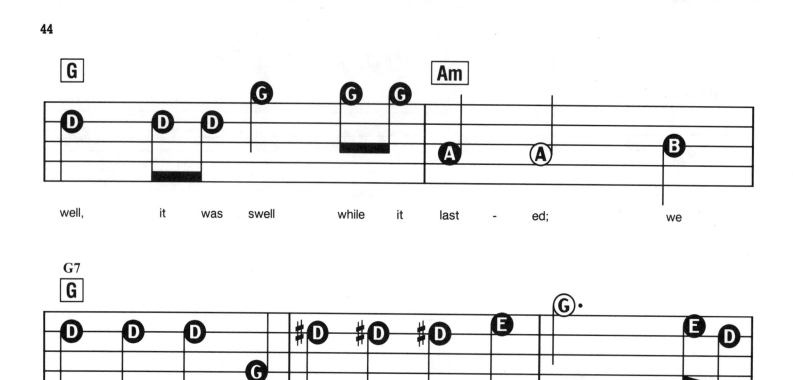

well, it was swell while it last - ed; we

did have fun and no harm done, and thanks for the

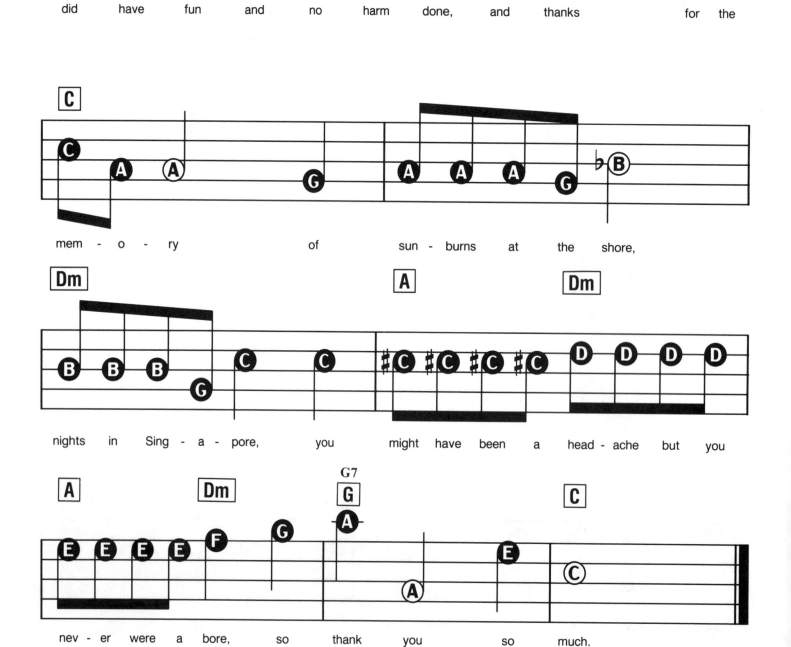

mem - o - ry of sun - burns at the shore,

nights in Sing - a - pore, you might have been a head - ache but you

nev - er were a bore, so thank you so much.

Two Sleepy People

Registration 4
Rhythm: Swing or Fox-Trot

Words by Frank Loesser
Music by Hoagy Carmichael

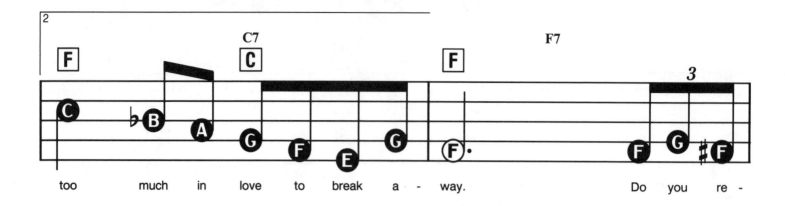

too much in love to break a - way. Do you re -

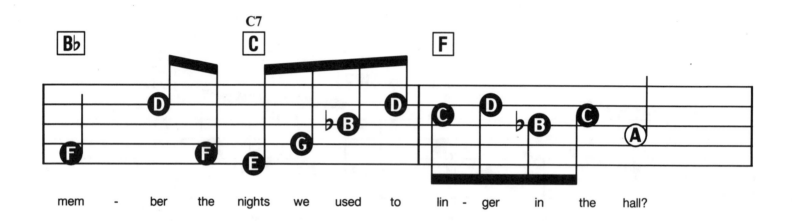

mem - ber the nights we used to lin - ger in the hall?

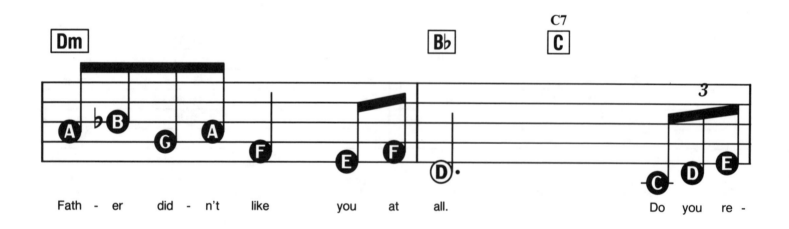

Fath - er did - n't like you at all. Do you re -

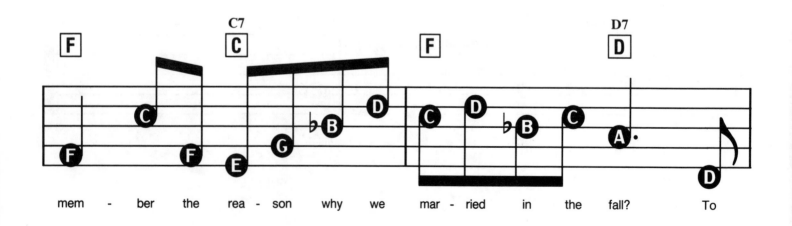

mem - ber the rea - son why we mar - ried in the fall? To

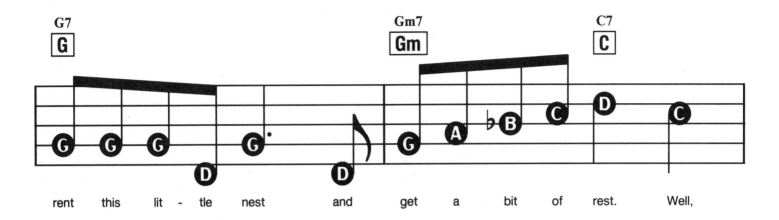

rent this lit - tle nest and get a bit of rest. Well,

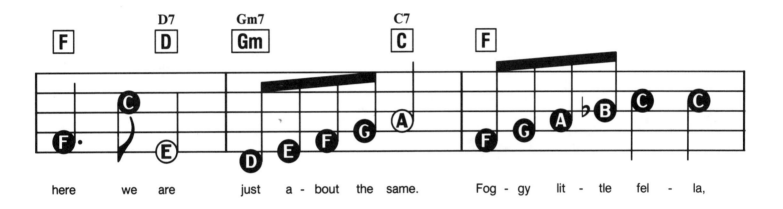

here we are just a - bout the same. Fog - gy lit - tle fel - la,

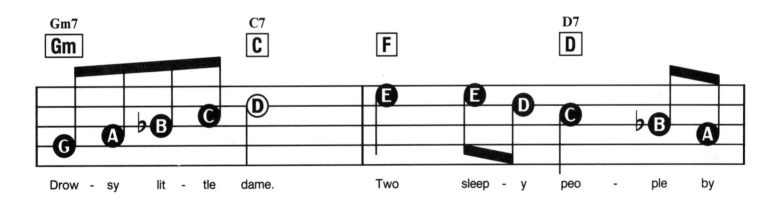

Drow - sy lit - tle dame. Two sleep - y peo - ple by

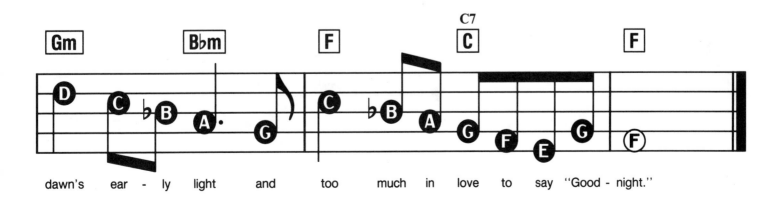

dawn's ear - ly light and too much in love to say "Good - night."

That's Amore

(That's Love)

Registration 3
Rhythm: Waltz

Words by Jack Brooks
Music by Harry Warren

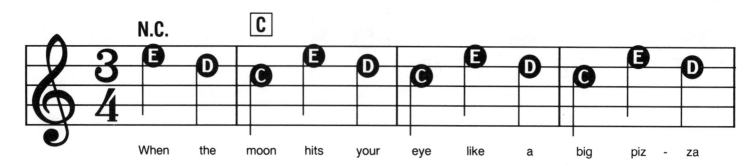

When the moon hits your eye like a big piz - za

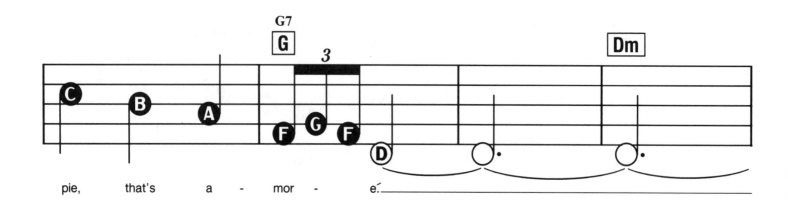

pie, that's a - mor - e.

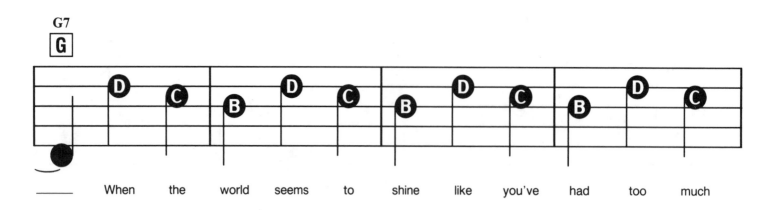

When the world seems to shine like you've had too much

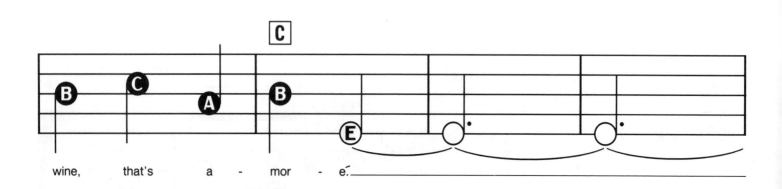

wine, that's a - mor - e.

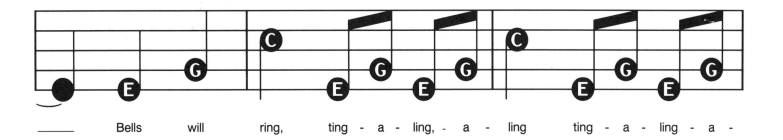

Bells will ring, ting - a - ling, - a - ling ting - a - ling - a -

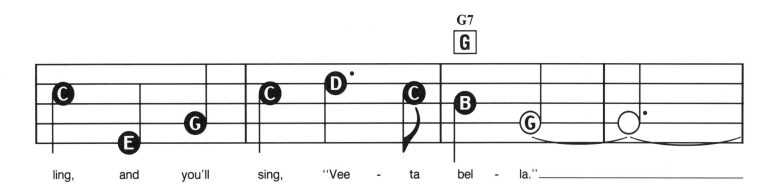

ling, and you'll sing, "Vee - ta bel - la." _____

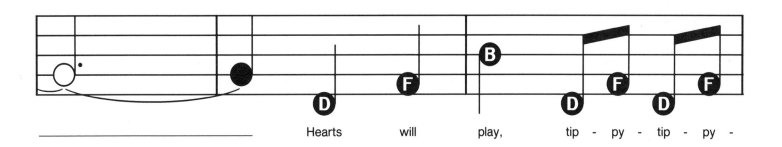

_____ Hearts will play, tip - py - tip - py -

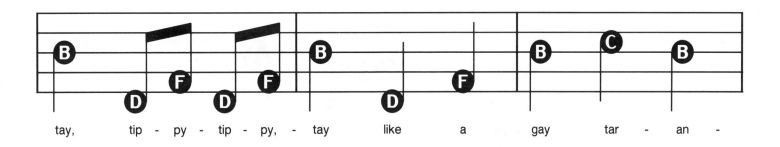

tay, tip - py - tip - py, - tay like a gay tar - an -

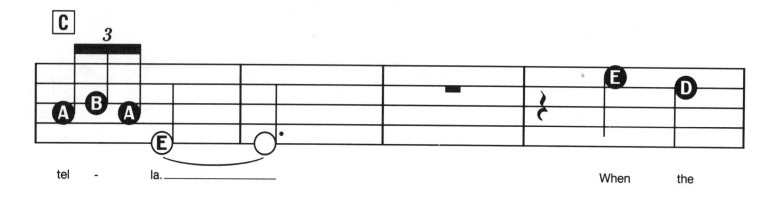

tel - la._____ When the

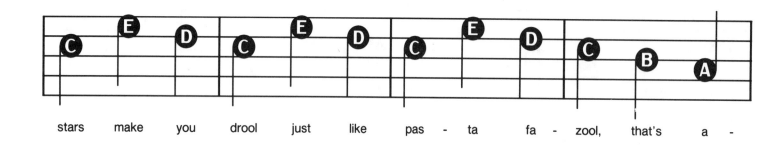

stars make you drool just like pas - ta fa - zool, that's a -

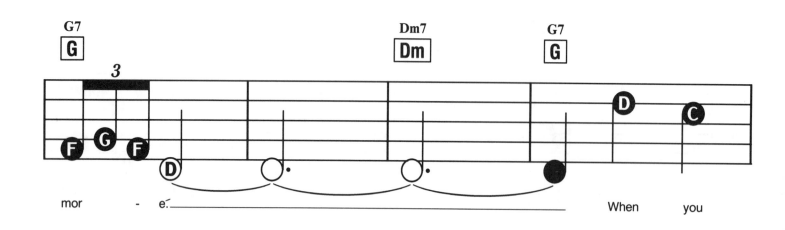

mor - e._____ When you

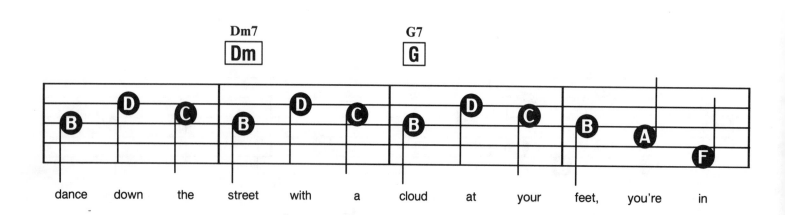

dance down the street with a cloud at your feet, you're in

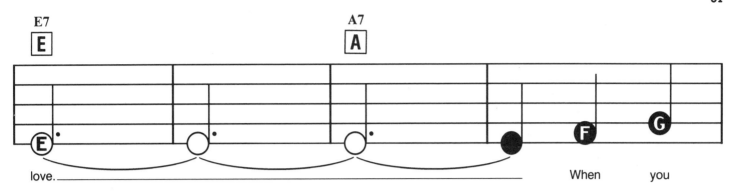

love._____ When you

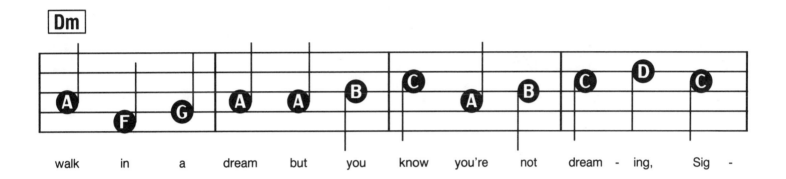

walk in a dream but you know you're not dream - ing, Sig -

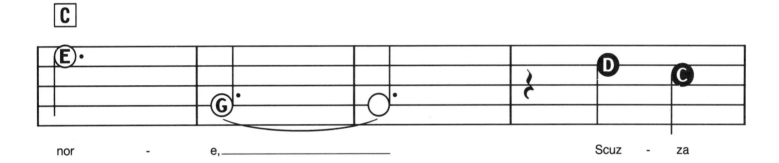

nor - e,_____ Scuz - za

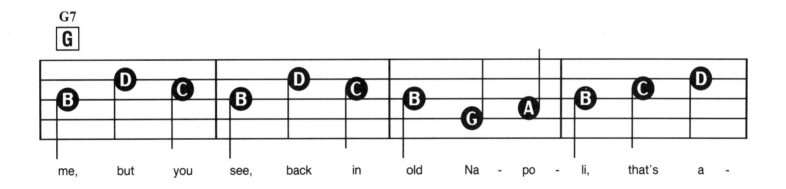

me, but you see, back in old Na - po - li, that's a -

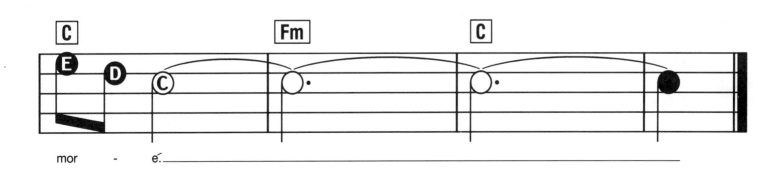

mor - é._____

This Is My Song

Registration 5
Rhythm: Fox Trot or Swing

By Charles Chaplin

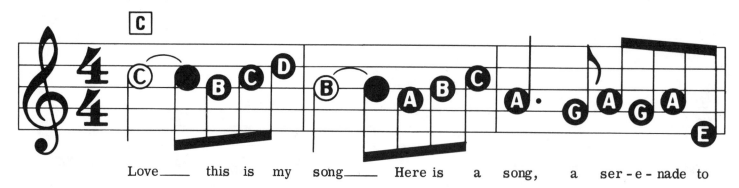

Love___ this is my song___ Here is a song, a ser-e-nade to

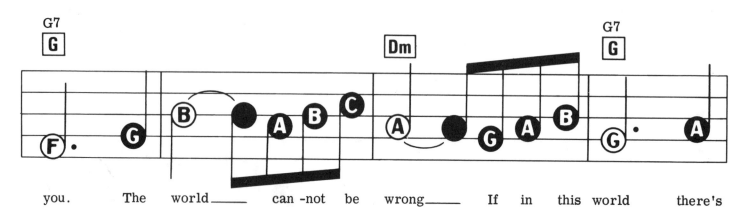

you. The world___ can-not be wrong___ If in this world there's

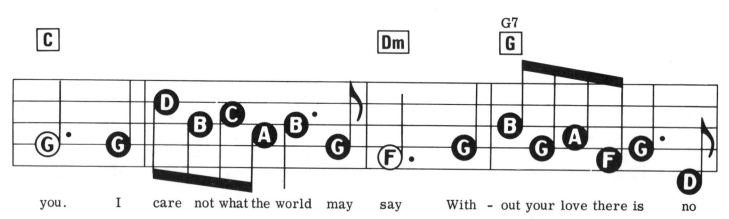

you. I care not what the world may say With-out your love there is no

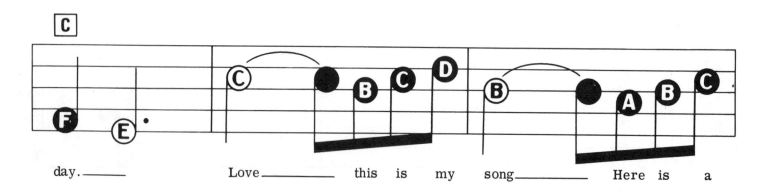

day.___ Love___ this is my song___ Here is a

MCA music publishing

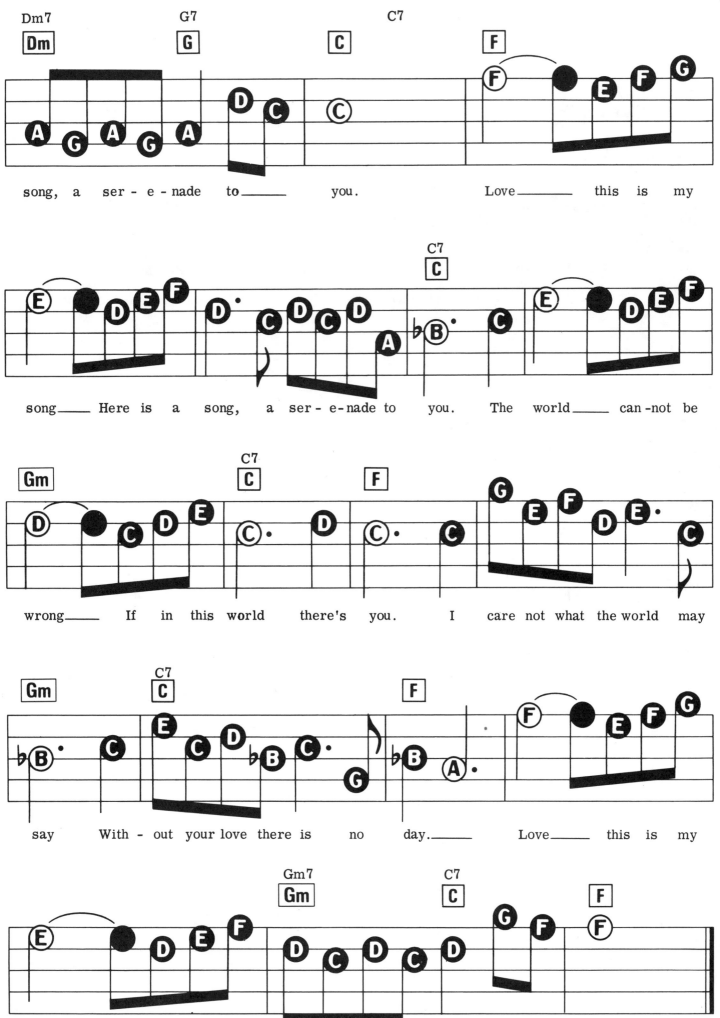

Undecided

Registration 7
Rhythm: Swing or Fox Trot

Words by Sid Robin
Music by Charles Shavers

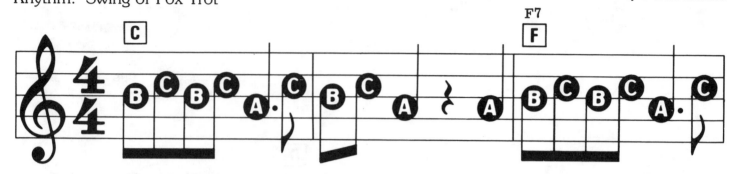

First you say you do and then you don't, and then you say you will and

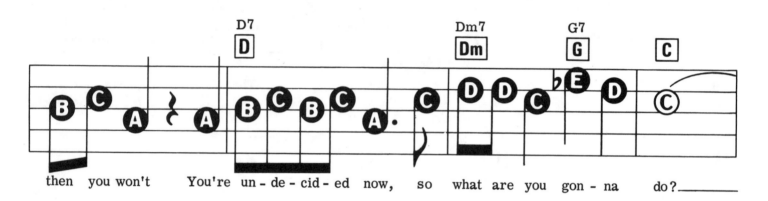

then you won't You're un - de - cid - ed now, so what are you gon - na do?_____

Now you want to play, and then it's no, and when you say you'll stay, that's

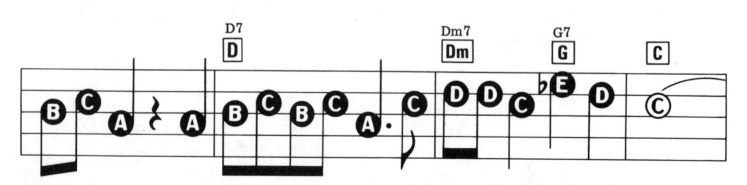

when you go. You're un - de - cid - ed now, so what are you gon - na do?_____

I've been sit-ting on a fence, and it does-n't make much sense, 'cause you

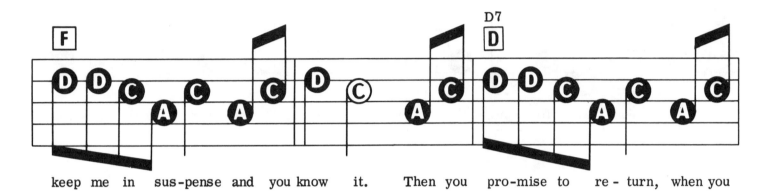

keep me in sus-pense and you know it. Then you pro-mise to re - turn, when you

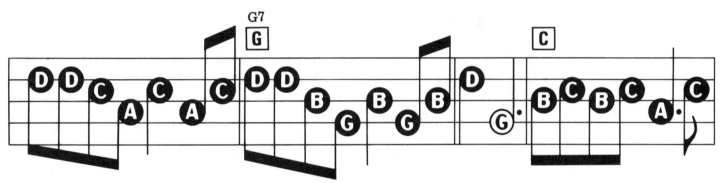

don't I real - ly burn, well, I guess I'll nev - er learn, and I show it. If you've got a heart and

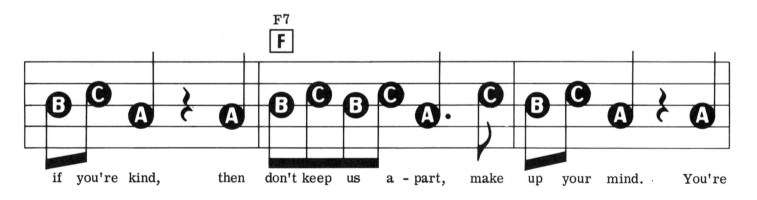

if you're kind, then don't keep us a - part, make up your mind. You're

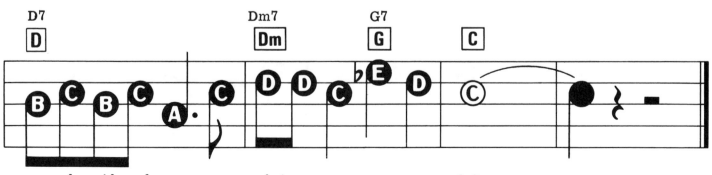

un - de - cid - ed now, so what are you gon - na do?_____

What A Diff'rence A Day Made

Registration 8
Rhythm: Latin or Rhumba

Lyric by Stanley Adams
Music by Maria Grever

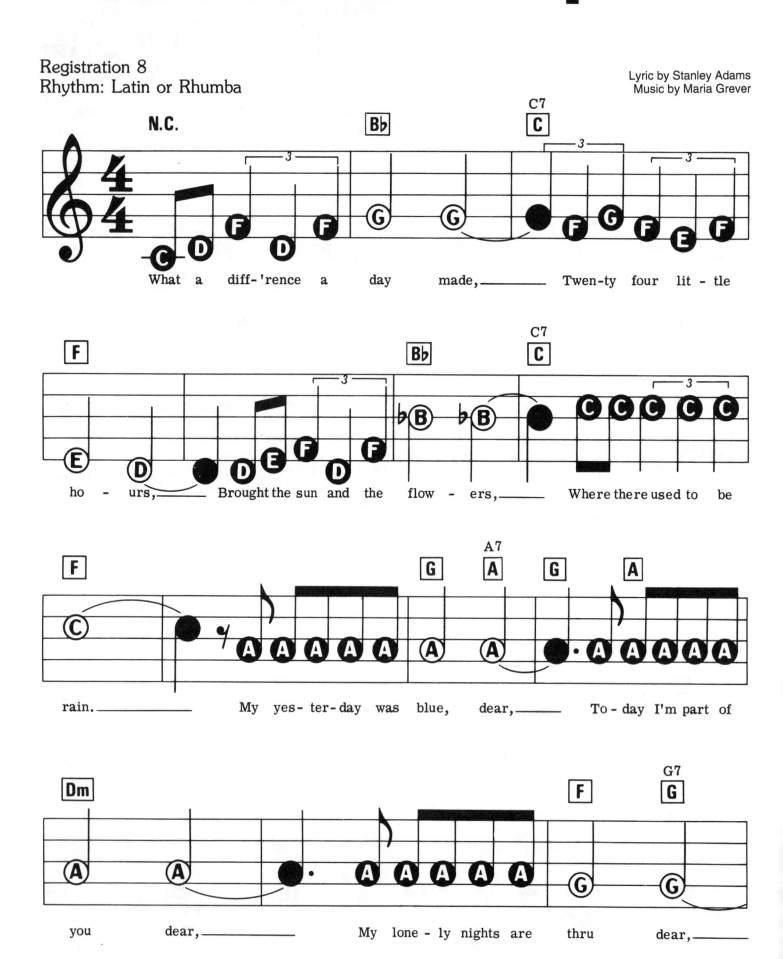

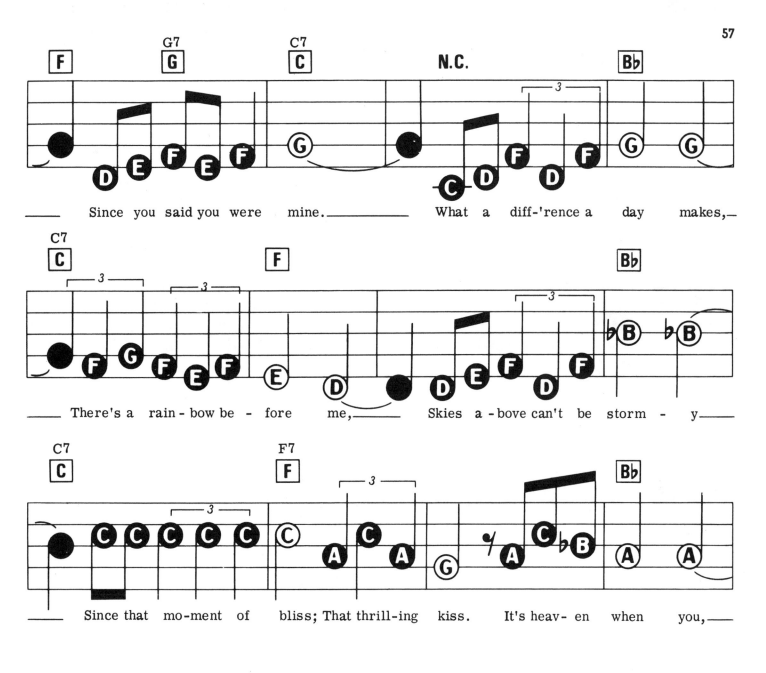

Since you said you were mine. What a diff-'rence a day makes,

There's a rain-bow be - fore me, Skies a -bove can't be storm - y

Since that mo-ment of bliss; That thrill-ing kiss. It's heav- en when you,

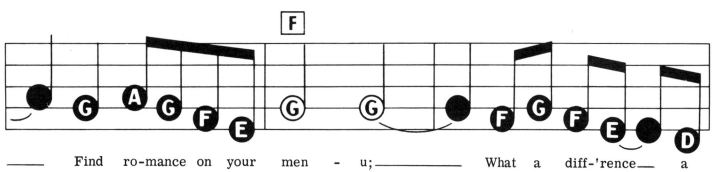

Find ro-mance on your men - u; What a diff-'rence a

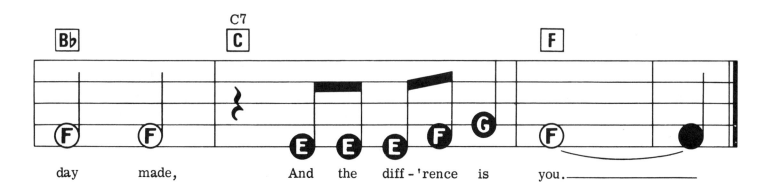

day made, And the diff -'rence is you.

When I Fall In Love

Registration 10
Rhythm: Fox Trot or Ballad

Words by Edward Heyman
Music by Victor Young

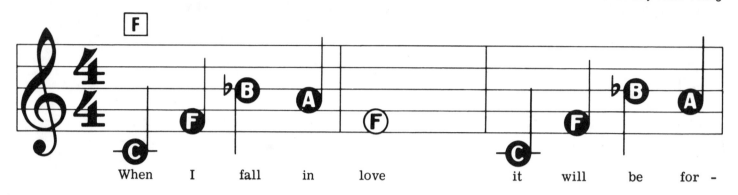

When I fall in love it will be for -

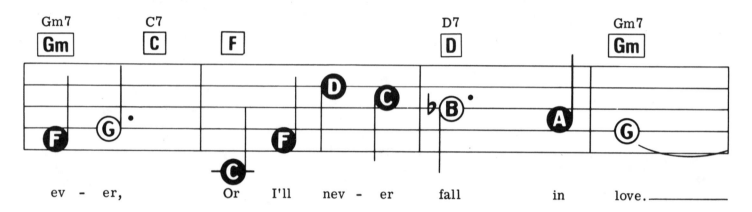

ev - er, Or I'll nev - er fall in love.

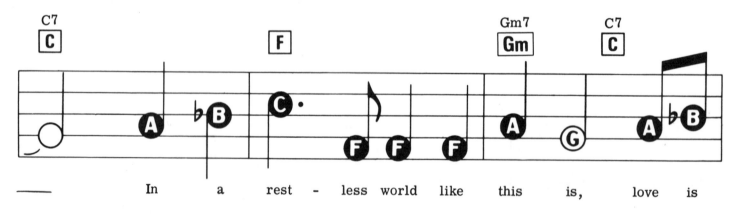

In a rest - less world like this is, love is

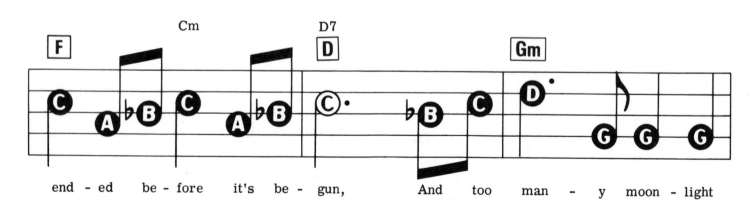

end - ed be - fore it's be - gun, And too man - y moon - light

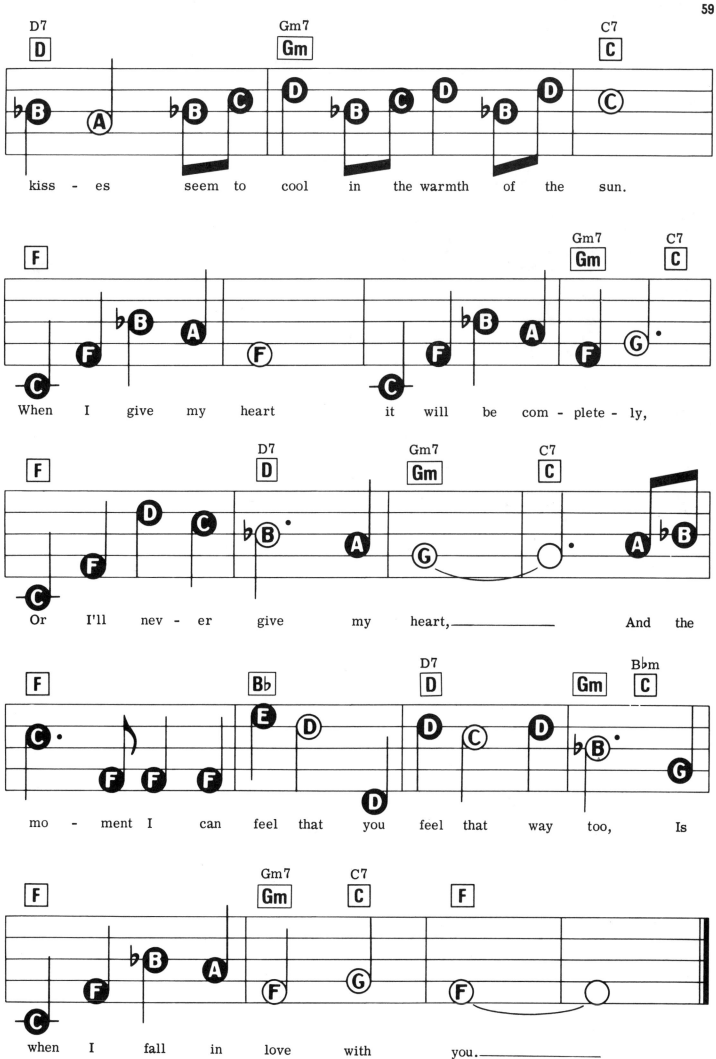

Where Is Your Heart
(The Song From Moulin Rouge)

Registration 9
Rhythm: Waltz

Words by William Engvick
Music by George Auric

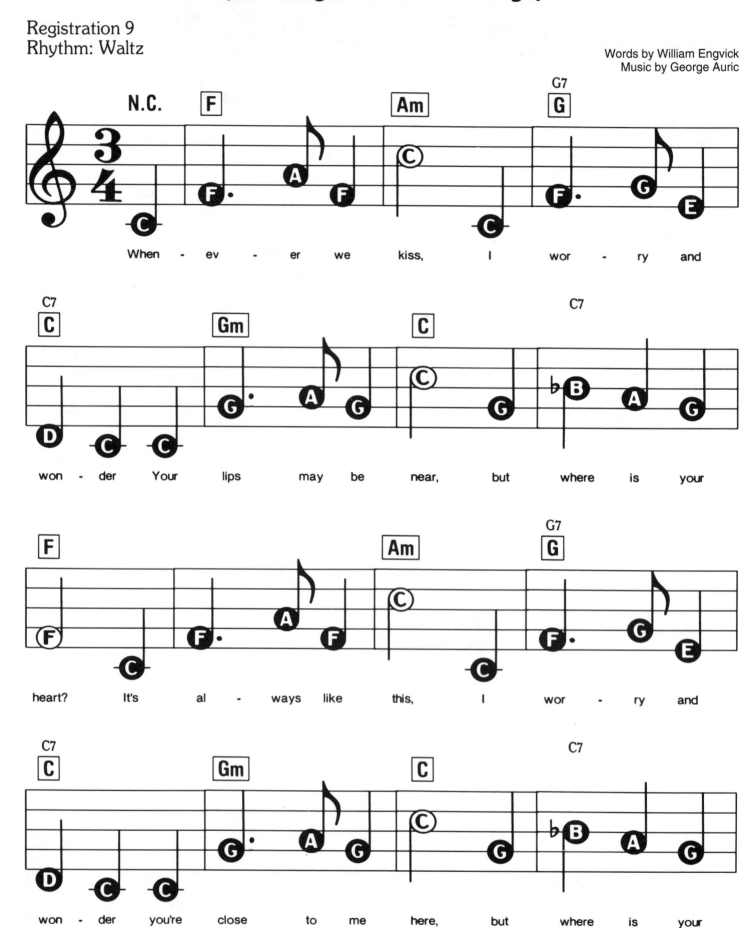

61

The Wonder Of You

Registration 4
Rhythm: Rock

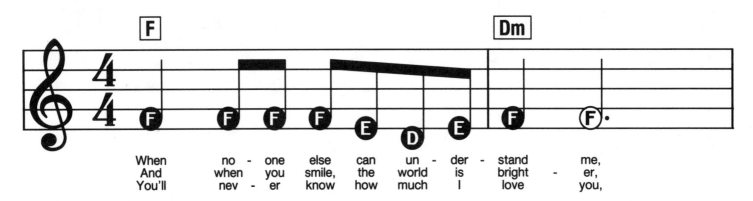

When no - one else can un - der - stand me,
And when you smile, the world is bright - er,
You'll nev - er know how much I love you,

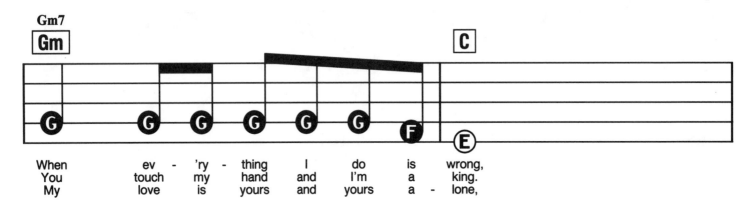

When ev - 'ry - thing I do is wrong,
You touch my hand and I'm a king.
My love is yours and yours a - lone,

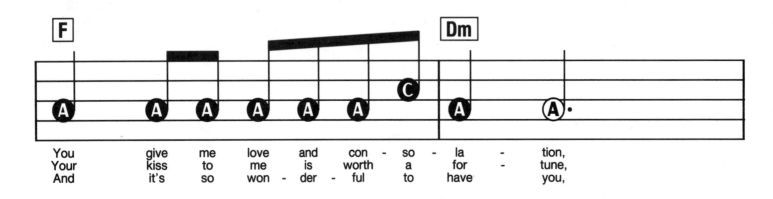

You give me love and con - so - la - tion,
Your kiss to me is worth a for - tune,
And it's so won - der - ful to have you,

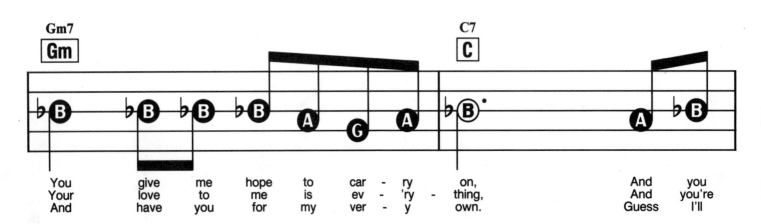

You give me hope to car - ry on,   And you
Your love to me is ev - 'ry - thing,   And you're
And have you for my ver - y own.   Guess I'll

MCA music publishing

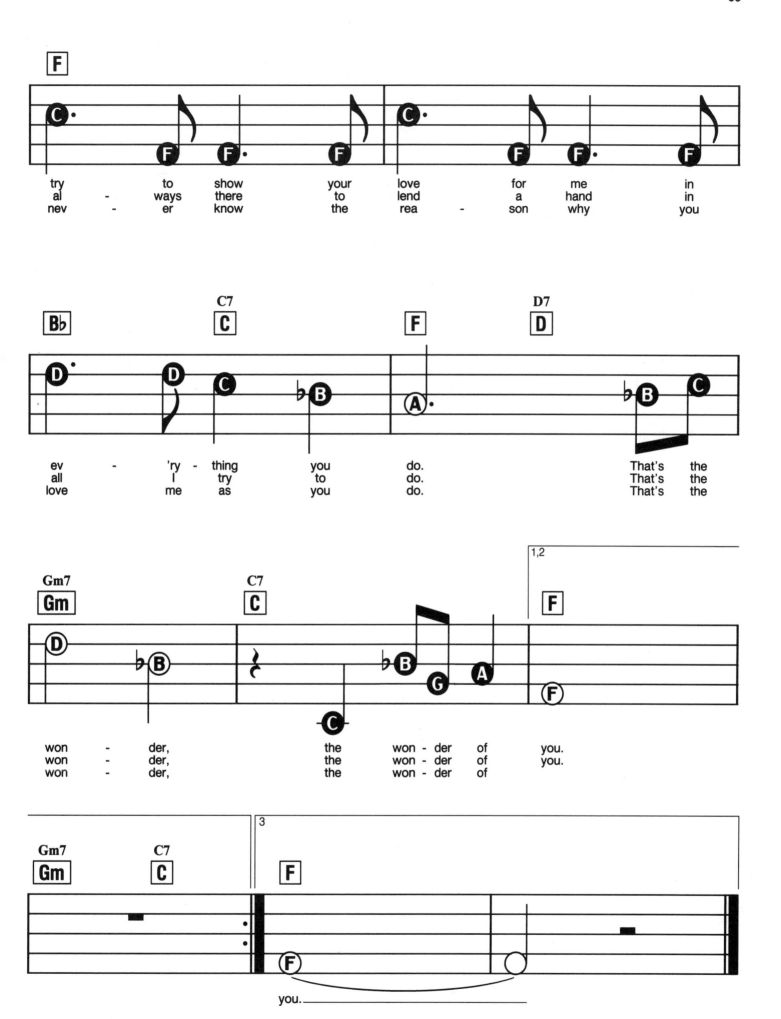

Registration Guide

- Match the Registration number on the song to the corresponding numbered category below. Select and activate an instrumental sound available on your instrument.

- Choose an automatic rhythm appropriate to the mood and style of the song. (Consult your Owner's Guide for proper operation of automatic rhythm features.)

- Adjust the tempo and volume controls to comfortable settings.

Registration

1	Flute, Pan Flute, Jazz Flute
2	Clarinet, Organ
3	Violin, Strings
4	Brass, Trumpet, Bass
5	Synth Ensemble, Accordion, Brass
6	Pipe Organ, Harpsichord
7	Jazz Organ, Vibraphone, Vibes, Electric Piano, Jazz Guitar
8	Piano, Electric Piano
9	Trumpet, Trombone, Clarinet, Saxophone, Oboe
10	Violin, Cello, Strings